THE PURE THEORY
OF FOREIGN TRADE

THE PURE THEORY ·
OF DOMESTIC VALUES

D1255586

THE PURE THEORY
OF FOREIGN TRADE

THE PURE THEORY
OF DOMESTIC VALUES

BY

ALFRED MARSHALL

[1930]

AUGUSTUS M. KELLEY • PUBLISHERS
CLIFTON 1974

Privately Printed 1879

First Published 1930

(*London*: The London School of Economics and
Political Science, University of London, *Houghton
Street, W. C. 2*, 1930)

Reprinted 1974 by

Augustus M. Kelley Publishers

Clifton New Jersey 07012

Library of Congress Cataloging in Publication Data

Marshall, Alfred, 1842-1924.
  The pure theory of foreign trade.

  (Reprints of economic classics)
  Reprint of the 1930 ed. published by the London
School of Economics and Political Science, London in:
Series of reprints of scarce tracts of economic and
political science.
    1. Commerce. 2. Value. 3. Economics, Mathemati-
cal. I. Title. II. Title: The pure theory of
domestic values. III. Series: Series of reprints of
scarce tracts of economic and political science.
HF1007.M35 1974   382   73-22013
ISBN 0-678-01194-X

PRINTED IN THE UNITED STATES OF AMERICA
by SENTRY PRESS, NEW YORK, N. Y. 10013
Bound by A. HOROWITZ & SON, CLIFTON, N. J.

EDITORIAL NOTE

THE circumstances under which these two essays were first printed is outlined by Alfred Marshall in a footnote to the preface of the first edition of his *Principles of Economics:*

> ". . . In 1875-7 I nearly completed a draft of a treatise on *The Theory of Foreign Trade, with some allied problems relating to the doctrine of Laisser Faire* . . . nearly all the diagrams that are now in Book V, Ch. V., VII and VIII were introduced in it . . . and there were others relating to Foreign Trade. . . . it is to them that Professor Sidgwick refers in the Preface to his *Political Economy.* With my consent he selected four chapters (not consecutive) out of the second Part, and printed them for private circulation. . . . They have been sent to many economists in England and on the Continent; it is of them that Jevons speaks in the Preface to the Second Edition of his *Theory* (p. xiv); and many of the diagrams in them relating to foreign trade have been reproduced with generous acknowledgments by Prof. Pantaleoni in his *Principii di Economia Pura.*"

It should also be noted that *Pure Theory of Domestic Values* provided the basis for Book III, Chapter VI of *Principles of Economics.* In a footnote to Appendix I of *Money Credit and Commerce* reference is made to *Pure Theory of International Trade:*

> "This Appendix is attached to Book III, Chapter VIII. Much of it had been designed to form part of an Appendix to a volume on International Trade . . . the main body of the present Appendix is reproduced with but little change in substance from that part of the MSS. which was privately printed and circulated among economists at home and abroad in 1879 . . ."

These essays were first reprinted in this series in 1930, from a copy lent by Mrs. Marshall. For the present reprinting, the Marshall Library, Cambridge, has lent a copy of the original edition. The diagrams have been redrawn and checked against the available copies of the original, and an editorial commentary has been added to the end of the volume.

G.S.D.

THE

PURE THEORY OF FOREIGN TRADE.

CHAPTER I.

THE PREMISES OF THE PURE THEORY OF FOREIGN TRADE. THE
METHOD OF DIAGRAMS. THE FUNDAMENTAL LAWS OF CURVES
WHICH REPRESENT INTERNATIONAL DEMAND.

THE function of a pure theory is to deduce definite conclusions from definite hypothetical premises. The premises should
approximate as closely as possible to the facts with which the
corresponding applied theory has to deal. But the terms used
in the pure theory must be capable of exact interpretation, and
the hypotheses on which it is based must be simple and easily
handled.

The pure theory of foreign trade satisfies these conditions.
This theory is based upon the hypothesis that two countries, say
England and Germany, carry on trade with each other but only
with each other. It is assumed that they are not under any
obligations to make foreign payments excepting those arising
from trade, so that in equilibrium the exports of each country
exchange for her imports. It is assumed that the pure theory
of domestic values has provided the means of measuring the
value in England of all the various wares exported by England in
terms of any one of them. Suppose cloth of a definite quality to be
one of them; then the value, in England, of all the wares which
England exports may be expressed as that of a certain number
of yards of cloth. So the value in Germany of all the wares
which Germany exports, may be expressed as that of, say, a
certain number of yards of linen.

We may for brevity use the phrase "a certain number of yards of cloth," as a substitute for the complete phrase "English wares the equivalent of a certain number of yards of cloth": and so for linen. Further we may consider that the processes of producing the cloth and the linen are not completed until the cloth and the linen are delivered in Germany and England respectively. By this means we shall avoid the necessity of specially mentioning the expenses of transport; so that we shall find no occasion to follow Mill in making the assumption that the expenses of transport may be neglected.

We may apply this method of speaking to express the conditions under which trade is in equilibrium; i.e. is such that there is no tendency for the imports and exports of the countries in question to increase or to diminish. Thus:—In equilibrium a certain number, say ten million, of yards of cloth are exported annually to Germany and sold there for a price which covers the expenses of producing a certain number, say fifteen million, of yards of linen. Vice versa, fifteen million yards of linen are exported to England and sold there for a price which covers the expense of producing ten million yards of cloth.

We are now in a position to give a definite interpretation to the phrase "the rate of interchange between two countries" in place of the inexact account sometimes given. We may measure the rate of interchange between England and Germany by the amount of linen which England obtains in return for each yard of cloth which she exports.

It seems on the whole best thus to represent the value of the wares which England exports as equivalent to that of a certain number of yards of cloth. But we might measure it as equivalent to a certain number of units of English capital and labour, or as we may say as equivalent to a certain number of units of English cost of production[1]. We should then measure the rate of interchange between England and Germany by the number of units of German cost of production which England obtains in return for the produce of a given number of units of her cost of production. This latter method of measurement has several advantages, and there is no reason why it should not be adopted in the treatment of some portions of the pure theory of foreign trade. But for the general purposes of the theory the method of measurement first given will be found to be the most convenient.

The theory of foreign trade is necessarily difficult. Mill when introducing it says, "I must give notice that we are now in the

---

[1] For a solution of the ambiguities connected with the use of this phrase see Appendix I.

region of the most complicated questions which Political Economy affords: that the subject is one which cannot possibly be made elementary; and that a more continuous effort of attention than has [in the earlier portions of the science] been required will be necessary in order to follow the series of deduction." The unavoidable difficulties of the subject are great: but students frequently fall into errors which they may easily avoid if they will resolve that when discussing the pure theory they will not speak of the imports or exports of a country as measured in terms of money.

Suppose that the fact to be expressed is that England has increased her demand for the wares of Germany; and has thereby caused the rate of interchange to be altered to her disadvantage.

It is found by experience that students commencing the subject have a tendency to describe this fact thus:—England used to import (say) ten million pounds worth of German wares, giving for them (after allowing for carriage) ten million pounds worth of English: but her demand for German wares increases so that she purchases twelve million pounds worth; and, the rate of interchange being altered to her disadvantage she has to give in return for them (after allowing for carriage) thirteen million pounds worth of her own wares.

This statement is inaccurate because it ignores the changes that will meanwhile have occurred in the standards of prices in the two countries. After, as well as before, the change in England's demand, each million pounds worth of English goods will be exchanged (allowance being made for the cost of carriage) for a million pounds worth of German goods, prices being measured according to the new standard. But the change will have caused gold to flow from England to Germany, so as to raise prices in Germany and lower them in England. So that the above statement should have been:—England imports an amount of German wares which according to the old standard of German prices was worth twelve million pounds, but according to the new standard of prices is worth (say) twelve and a half millions. In exchange England exports an amount of her own wares which according to the old standard of her prices was worth thirteen million pounds, but according to the new standard is worth twelve and a half millions. This statement is accurate but uselessly complex. And the complexities of which this is an instance, increase till they become wholly unmanageable if the attempt is made to proceed far into the pure theory of foreign trade on the plan of measuring exports and imports in terms of money.

§ 2. We may now proceed to consider the laws which govern the demand of one country for the wares of another. The explanation of these laws is tolerably simple, so long as we are dealing only with the normal conditions of foreign trade. Under ordinary circumstances, a decrease in a country's exports will cause her to obtain her imports on terms more advantageous, but not much more advantageous than before. There will be increased competition for her wares in foreign markets, and consequently their price will tend to rise; but as some at least of her wares will be closely pressed by the rivalry of foreign producers, the rate of interchange will not be altered in her favour sufficiently to prevent a decrease in the amount of her imports. Similarly any increase in her exports will cause her to obtain an increase in her imports, though she will obtain them on somewhat less advantageous terms. So long, then, as we assume these normal conditions to exist, we may trace the changes of foreign trade by means of the ordinary processes of general reasoning, without the aid of any artificial apparatus. But such a treatment becomes very difficult, if not impossible, when we pass to consider exceptional cases in which these normal conditions fail: and it is the special task of the pure theory of foreign trade to deal with such exceptional cases. The only apparatus which Ricardo and Mill brought to bear on the problems of pure economic theory was that of arithmetical illustration. But this is inadequate to the work. The use of numerical examples will perhaps enable the investigator to ascertain some of the consequences which may arise from the causes into whose operation he is inquiring: but it affords no security that he will discover all of these consequences or even the most important of them. Moreover when he has deduced certain conclusions from a particular set of numbers which he has chosen to illustrate certain general premises, he is not unlikely to infer that these conclusions follow necessarily from the premises he has laid down: whereas these conclusions may be latent in the particular choice of numbers that he has made, and may not be capable of being deduced from every set of numbers which satisfy the conditions laid down in the general premises. Experience proves that even powerful thinkers are liable to be thus led into error in spite of their being well aware that the legitimate use of numerical examples is only to illustrate and not to prove general rules. The weakness and inefficiency of this apparatus will be demonstrated in the course of the present examination of the theory of foreign trade. For the free use of numerical examples has not enabled Ricardo and Mill to discover the conclusions which follow necessarily from their hypothesis.

The pure theory of economic science requires the aid of an apparatus which can grasp and handle the general quantitative relations on the assumption of which the theory is based. The most powerful engines for such a purpose are supplied by the various branches of mathematical calculus. But diagrams are of great service, wherever they are applicable, in interpreting to the eye the processes by which the methods of mathematical analysis obtain their results. It happens that with a few unimportant exceptions all the results which have been obtained by the application of mathematical methods to pure economic theory can be obtained independently by the method of diagrams.

Diagrams present simultaneously to the eye the chief forces which are at work, laid out, as it were, in a map; and thereby suggest results to which attention has not been directed by the use of the methods of mathematical analysis. The method of diagrams can be freely used by every one who is capable of exact reasoning, even though he have no knowledge of Mathematics. The reader, who will take the trouble to assure himself that he thoroughly understands the account of the curves given in the following paragraphs, will not find difficulty in following the reasoning to which they are afterwards applied.

§ 3. The most convenient mode of procedure will be to commence by examining the conditions of the first of the exceptional cases to which ·reference has been made; then to interpret the normal conditions of the problem as well as these exceptional conditions into the language of diagrams; and afterwards to treat the second exceptional case, which is of minor importance.

The first exceptional case is that of a group of problems in which it is assumed that a diminution of the total exports of a country may cause these to be in such urgent demand abroad that she obtains in return for her diminished exports an increased instead of a diminished supply of foreign wares. The results of an investigation of this exceptional case are capable of being applied in the partial and indirect solution of some practical problems connected with the trade that is carried on between existing countries; particularly in connexion with duties on exportation. But the chief importance of these results arises from the fact that they may be applied to the trade that a compact industrial group carries on with its neighbours. We shall refer to this class of problems as "Class I."; and shall give the name of "Class II." to the second exceptional case to which reference has been made; the case, namely, in which an increase in the amount of wares which a country produces for exportation effects a very great diminution in the expenses at which she can produce them ; so that the consequent fall in their value diminishes the total amount of the imports that she receives in exchange for them. When we are considering the circumstances of trade from which both these exceptional cases are excluded, we may for brevity say that we are discussing the " Normal class" of problems.

Applying this classification to the special case of the trade in cloth and linen which we have supposed to be carried on between England and Germany, we may say :—Every increase in the amount of linen which is thrown annually on the English market will necessitate a cheapening of the terms on which it is offered for sale. The effect of this cheapening will (save in problems of Class II.) cause each yard of linen to exchange for the means of producing and exporting a smaller amount of cloth than before : that is, will alter the rate of interchange in England's favour[1]. In the Normal Class this alteration will be slight, so that every increase in the amount of linen imported will occasion an increase in the amount of cloth exported. But in Class I. an increase in the amount of linen imported will depress the price at which it can be sold in England, and it will alter the rate of interchange in England's favour to so great an extent as to cause the amount of cloth exported not to increase but diminish. A precisely similar statement of course applies to Germany's demand for cloth. Class I. may be illustrated numerically thus :—Suppose the sale of 10 million yards of linen in England to afford the means of purchasing and exporting 10 million yards of cloth, the rate of interchange being thus, one yard of cloth to one yard of linen. An increase in the amount of linen to 15 million yards may perhaps cause the amount of cloth to increase to 12 million : while it is possible that a further increase in the linen to 20 million may so force down its price in the English market as to cause the rate of interchange to become two yards of linen for one of cloth ; in which case the amount of cloth which Germany obtains will fall to ten million yards.

§ 4. Let us now commence to interpret the laws of international demand into the language of diagrams. Let distances measured along a fixed straight line Ox (fig. 1) represent numbers of yards of cloth. Let distances measured along a straight line Oy at right angles to Ox represent numbers of yards of linen. Let a curve OE be drawn as follows :—N being any point upon Oy, let it be determined from a knowledge of the

---

[1] An examination of extraordinary circumstances in which this may not be true will be found in §§ 5, 6.

circumstances of England's demand for linen, what is the number of yards of cloth, the expenses of producing and exporting which will be covered annually by the proceeds of the sale in England of an amount of linen represented by ON. From Ox measure off OM, equal to this number of yards of cloth. Draw lines through M and N at right angles to Ox and Oy respectively, meeting in P; then P is a point on the required curve, OE. If N be moved from O gradually along Oy, P will assume a series of positions, each of which corresponds to one position of N; the continuous string of points thus formed will be the curve OE. [In other words, OE will be the locus of P.] If we were applying the method of diagrams to the trade that is actually carried on between two countries, we could not indeed obtain trustworthy data for drawing more than a limited portion of the curve. For it is not possible to conjecture with any approach to certainty what would be the terms on which it would be possible to sell in a country an amount of imports, either very much greater, or very much less, than that which is actually sold there. But for the purposes of the pure theory we are at liberty to suppose that the curve is properly drawn throughout its entire length. We may call OE "England's demand curve;" and bearing in mind that PM is equal to ON, we may describe it thus :—

England's demand curve is such that any point P being taken on it, and PM *being drawn perpendicular to* Ox *;* OM *represents the amount of cloth which England will be willing to give annually for an amount of linen represented by* PM.

In exactly the same way we may construct a curve OG which may be called Germany's demand curve, and which may be described thus :—

Germany's demand curve is such that any point p being taken upon it and pm *being drawn perpendicular to* Ox *;* pm *represents the amount of linen which Germany will be willing to give annually for an amount of cloth represented by* Om.

It may not be superfluous to state explicitly that the period for which the supplies of cloth and linen are reckoned is taken as a year only, for the purposes of definiteness and brevity. If the phrase "in a given unit of time" were not cumbrous, it might be substituted throughout for the word "annually."

The terms in which the curves are described imply that there is no change in the circumstances which govern the amount of linen that England is willing to take at each particular rate of interchange : and similarly that the circumstances which govern the German demand for cloth remain constant. As a matter of fact the causes which govern the demand of a country for foreign wares do vary from time to time. They are altered by

every change that affects her power of raising on the one hand
the wares which she exports, and on the other domestic rivals
to the wares which she imports; by almost every invention,
and almost every change of fashion. But, as has been already
said, we should aim at simplicity in our first approximations, in
order that they may be easily manageable. Therefore, we are
to neglect for the present all consideration of the disturbances
arising from such variations; leaving account to be taken of
them in the applications of the results of the pure theory to
practical issues.

§ 5. We may now interpret into the language of curves
the laws of international demand. The first proposition to be
laid down requires no proof. It is that corresponding to every

The laws statement that can be made with regard to·the terms on which
of the two England may be willing to export cloth in exchange for linen,
curves are there is a similar statement with regard to the terms on which
symmetri-
cal. Germany may be willing to import linen in exchange for cloth.
Or in other words :—

PROP. I. *Every statement as to the shape which it is possible
for* OE *to assume, has corresponding to it a similar statement as
to the shape which it is possible for* OG *to assume ; but wherever*
Ox *occurs in the former statement,* Oy *will occur in the latter,
and vice versa ; whenever reference is made to a horizontal straight
line in the former, there must be made reference in the latter to a
vertical straight line, and vice versa.*

If the reader should be unaccustomed to such a process of
substitution, he may be helped to realize its validity, if he will
draw any one of the figures that belong to the pure theory of
foreign trade, with a broad pen on thin paper. He should then
hold the paper between him and the light, with the reverse of
the paper to him, with Oy horizontal, and Ox pointing vertically upwards. He will see through the paper, the two curves
OE and OG with their places interchanged. Whatever proposition the figure has been used to prove with regard to OE, will
now apply without any change or substitution to OG; when he
has gone through this proof, he may turn the figure back again
to its old position. He will observe that this proposition does
not affirm that in any particular state of the trade, the shape of
OG will be similar to the shape of OE: but only that whatever
be the limits within which the possible variations in the shape
of OE are confined by the fundamental laws of foreign trade,
there exist precisely similar limits for OG.

It will suffice therefore to examine at length the laws which
Laws re- relate to the shape of OE. We may first lay down some laws
lating to which hold in the Normal Class and Class I., but not in
the Nor- Class II.

Let us suppose N to move from O along Oy, and let us mal Class and Class I. watch the corresponding changes in the magnitude of OM and in the ratio of ON to OM. We find :—

PROP. II. *For the Normal Class and Class I.*: *if* P *be a point moving along* OE, *and* PM, PN *drawn perpendicular to* Ox *and* Oy *respectively, every increase in* PM *is accompanied by an increase in the ratio of* PM *to* OM.

For the greater the amount of linen that has to be disposed of annually in England, the less will be the general purchasing power over which each yard of it will give command: and therefore, the less the amount of cloth that will be given in exchange for each yard of linen. The only exception to this is in the problems of Class II., in which an increase in the amount of cloth made for exportation may conceivably so increase the economy of its production as to enable a yard of cloth to be obtained by a less amount of general purchasing power than before. From this proposition we obtain at once,

PROP. III. *In curves of the Normal Class and of Class I. if* P *be any point in* OE, *every point in that portion of* OE *which is between* O *and* P *must lie below the straight line* OP; *and every point in the remaining portion of* OE *must lie above the straight line* OP *produced. Similarly if* p *be any point in* OG *every point in that portion of* OG *which is between* O *and* P *must lie to the left of the line* Op, *and every point in the remaining portion of* OG *must lie to the right of the straight line* Op *produced.* Hence we obtain at once,

PROP. IV. *If either of the curves belongs to the Normal Class or to Class I. it cannot cut twice any straight line through* O.

This result may be expressed in another form which will A geo-metrical expression for the rate of interchange. be more convenient for some purposes thus :

Let P be a point such that PM being drawn perpendicular to Ox, PM is the amount of linen which Germany is actually sending to England at any time in exchange for OM cloth. (We shall hereafter (see Ch. II.) call this point P the "Exchange-index.") Then the rate of interchange is indicated by the ratio between PM and OM. This ratio will be constant whatever position P may have on any given straight line through O. So that the rate of interchange is determined by the magnitude of the angle which the straight line joining P and O makes with Ox[1]: the greater this angle is, the more advantageous the

---

[1] It is measured mathematically by tan POx from the point of view of England, and by cot POx from the point of view of Germany. The mathematical reader will observe that in the Normal Case and in Case I. the curves may have points of contrary flexure. That is, if $y = f(x)$ be the equation to OE, $f''(x)$ may change sign at any point of the curve. But $\dfrac{d}{dy}\left(\dfrac{y}{x}\right)$ must remain positive:

rate of interchange is to England, and the less advantageous it is to Germany. Therefore Prop. IV. may be put in the form,

PROP. IV. COR. *If the demand curve of a country belong to the Normal Class or to Class I., the amount of foreign wares which she will import is determined when the rate of interchange is known.*

Again, in the Normal Class and in Class I. when the amount of linen offered for sale in England is very small, it will be disposed of on terms advantageous to Germany, so that the amount of cloth exported in exchange for it will be proportionally large. Thus where PM is small, the ratio of PM to OM is small: and a point moving from O along OE will keep at first close to Ox. So a point moving from O along OG will keep at first close to Oy.

It can hence be inferred, or it can be proved directly from Prop. IV., that—

PROP. V. *In the Normal Class and in Class I. that portion of* OE *which is adjacent to* O *lies below that portion of* OG *which is adjacent to* O.

Thus we may not invert the positions which OE and OG have in fig. (1) in the neighbourhood of O.

Under Class II. we shall have to discuss the forms which OE may assume if the production of cloth on a large scale for exportation renders possible important economies that would otherwise be impossible. But however extensive these economies may be, they cannot cause the total expenses of producing any given amount of cloth to be less than the total expenses of producing a smaller amount. Hence the general condition of the arts of production being assumed, we know definitely the expenses of producing any given amount of cloth in England for exportation.

Therefore OE cannot bend downwards towards Ox after the manner of the curve in fig. (2). For if OE could assume a shape such that a horizontal line AB could be drawn cutting it in A and B; then, AC and BD being drawn perpendicular to Ox, the shape of the curve would imply the following statement:—AC linen is just capable of being sold for the expenses of producing OC cloth: and also BD linen (which is the same as AC linen) is capable of being sold for the expenses of producing OD cloth. But this is impossible. Thus we obtain a fundamental law which is valid for the Normal Class and for

---

i.e. $x - y \dfrac{dx}{dy}$ must remain positive; i.e. every straight line which touches OE must cut Ox to the right of O. There is an obvious geometrical proof of this result.

Classes I. and II. and is the only law to which the curves must conform under all circumstances : viz.

PROP. VI.   OE *cannot in any case be cut more than once by a horizontal line.   Similarly* OG *cannot in any case be cut more than once by a vertical line.*

§ 6.   Let us next investigate the laws which bind the curves if they belong to the Normal Class, but not if they belong to Class I.   For the Normal Class, but not for Class I. it is assumed that every increase in the amount of linen offered for sale annually in England increases the total proceeds of the sale, and consequently increases the amount of cloth that is exported in exchange for it.   That is to say: if from N any point in Oy, NP be drawn at right angles to Oy to meet the curve OE in P, then the greater be ON the greater also is NP. But in Class I., as N moves from O along Oy the increase in ON though it is at first accompanied by an increase in NP, yet when N arrives at a certain point (V in fig. 3) NP ceases to increase and begins to diminish, and the curve bends round towards Oy.   These and corresponding results may be put in the following convenient form :

PROP. VII.   *In the Normal Class* OE *cannot cut the same vertical line more than once: but it may in Class I.   So in the Normal Class* OG *cannot cut the same horizontal line more than once; but it may in Class I.*

In fig. 3 the curves cut one another only in one point; but consistently with the conditions of Class I. they may cut one another several times, as represented in fig. 4.   It may be well formally to prove that—

PROP. VIII.   *In the Normal Class* OE *and* OG *cannot cut one another in more than one point (besides* O).

Let A be a point of intersection of the curves (see fig. 1); then AE must lie entirely above OA produced, by Prop. IV.; and AG must lie entirely to the right of OA produced: consequently AE and AG cannot cut again.   Nor can AE cut the portion of OG which lies between O and A.   For by Prop. VI. the portion of OG between O and A must lie entirely to the left of a vertical straight line through A; and by Prop. VII. AE must lie entirely to the right of this straight line.   Similarly AG cannot cut the portion of OE which lies between O and A. Therefore OE and OG cannot meet except in O and A.

PROP. IX.   *Every point in which the two curves cut one another corresponds to an equilibrium of the trade.*

Let AH, BK, CL be drawn perpendicular to Ox.   Then since A is a point on OE, AH linen can be sold annually in the English market for a price which will just cover the expenses of producing (and exporting to Germany) OH cloth: and since A is a point on OG, OH cloth can be sold annually in the German market for a price which will just cover the expenses of producing (and importing to England) AH linen. That is, when OH cloth is exchanged for AH linen, there is no force present either to increase or diminish England's exports or imports: trade is in equilibrium. A precisely similar proof shews that trade is in equilibrium when OK cloth is exchanged for BK linen. In the following chapter it will be proved that the equilibrium of the trade is *stable* in each of the positions represented by A in fig. (3) and by A and C in fig. (4): but that it is unstable in the position represented by B in fig. (4). The possibility of more than one position of equilibrium in such cases as this has been noticed by Mill. His treatment of the matter is certainly inadequate: for he has failed to discover the laws which determine whether any particular position of equilibrium is stable or unstable. It is, generally speaking, true of Mill as of Adam Smith, that much of his work which appears at first sight to contain error, proves itself on further investigation to be only incomplete or incompletely expressed. This is however one of the few instances in which careful study has failed to convince me that Mill's work is right as far as it goes. The reader who may care to inquire into this matter is referred to the Note at the end of the present chapter.

§ 7. We may proceed to the discussion of problems of Exceptional Class II. The case does not yet appear to have much direct bearing on questions relating either to the trade that is actually carried on between existing countries, or to the terms on which any compact industrial group is able to sell its wares or its services. But it claims attention on the ground that it is not logically excluded by the hypothesis on which the pure theory of foreign trade has been constructed since the time of Ricardo. Moreover history shews that the practical applications of the work of pure science have in general been discovered after, and not before, that work was done; advances in that applied knowledge which gives us direct command over nature have never been made with rapidity except when men have been willing to expend some pains on completing the solution of problems suggested to them by pure science, even although the practical purposes which the various portions of their work would subserve could not be discovered beforehand. Finally no great amount of additional trouble will be involved in working out this exceptional case.

This case has its origin in the fact that the wares which a country exports may be such that the difficulty of producing them diminishes very rapidly when their amount increases. It is indeed true, as has been said, that in general the production

of a commodity on a large scale for home consumption precedes
the development of any considerable foreign trade in it.   Still
the extent to which division of labour in the production of it can
be carried, is enlarged by every extension of the foreign markets
for it.   For instance, there exist in England large groups of
works each of which groups is filled with expensive machinery
that is adapted exclusively for making the special machinery
that is required in some one class of manufactures, and the
growth of such works has been very greatly promoted by foreign
trade.   Adam Smith mentioned as one of the chief advantages
of foreign trade that "by means of it the narrowness of the
home market does not hinder the division of labour in any
particular branch of art or manufacture from being carried to
the highest perfection."   And it is certain that in the century
which has followed the publication of Adam Smith's work
England's export trade has exerted a quiet but constant
influence in developing broad inventions and economies in
manufacture.   These have benefited foreign countries in the
first instance by causing England to sell them her manufactured
goods on cheap terms, and in the second instance by passing
over to those countries and assisting them to manufacture for
themselves.

Thus it is possible, to revert to our old hypothesis, that an
increase in Germany's demand for English cloth may to so great
an extent develope the facilities which England has for producing cloth as to cause a great and permanent fall in the value
of cloth in England.   It is true that in order to obtain this cloth
Germany will have in general to force a sale here for an increased amount of her own products, and consequently to lower
their price.   But it is conceivable that under exceptional conditions the increase in the amount of English cloth required for
exportation to Germany may cause an increase in the economy
of producing cloth so rapid and extensive that the fall in the
price of cloth in England may be greater than the fall in the
price of linen.   Thus it is possible that an increase in Germany's
demand for English cloth may cause each yard of linen to be
sold here on such terms as to give command over a larger
amount of cloth than before; it is possible that an increase in
Germany's demand for English cloth may cause her to obtain
an import of English cloth increased *in a greater ratio* than
is her export of linen to England.

The introduction of the economies which were requisite in
order to render possible such cases as this on a large scale have
seldom been effected within a short space of time.   The lapse
of generations has been required for that development of
England's invention and economies in manufacture which was

above attributed in part to her export trade. And the practical importance of such cases as have occurred on a somewhat small scale is in general less than at first sight appears. Let us examine one such case. The agricultural implements which England makes for herself are not always adapted for use in countries where the population is sparse. Eastern Europe wants field steam engines in which straw can be used as fuel; she wants mowing and reaping machines that can be used on uneven ground. Special knowledge, special skill and special machinery are to a greater or less extent required for the manufacture of these implements. For some time England played a very poor part in the work; partly because she had to compete with America who had organised this manufacture for her own market. At length the steady increase in the volume of the demand for these implements is enabling Englishmen to produce them with rapidly increasing economy. But their present success arises in great measure from their having had experience in the manufacture of wares of similar kind; and the main body of the work in which this experience has been obtained, is directed to the supply of the home market.

Let us proceed to interpret problems of Class II. in the language of diagrams. Let P, Q (fig. 5) be two points on $O. E.$ such that PM and QR being drawn perpendicular to Ox, QR is greater than PM. We found that in the Normal Class and in Class I. the ratio of QR to OR must be greater than the ratio of PM to OM (Prop. II.). But in Class II. it is possible for an increase in the amount of cloth produced in England so to diminish the expenses of producing each yard, that an increase in the amount of linen imported although it will cause the value of each yard of linen in England to fall, may yet cause each yard of linen to give the means of purchasing a greater amount of cloth than before: so that the exports of cloth increase not in a less ratio, but in a greater ratio than the imports of linen. So that the ratio of QR to OR may be less than the ratio of PM to OM. Hence,

PROP. X. *In Class II. the curves do not necessarily conform to the laws which are enunciated in Prop. II. III. IV. V. and VI. as valid for the Normal Class and for Class I.*

Thus for instance OE and OG may lie as in fig. 5; and may cut each other at A, B and C. The proof given in Prop. IX. that every point of intersection of the curves corresponds to a position of equilibrium of the trade applies to this case. It will be proved in the next chapter that A and C correspond to stable, and B to unstable, equilibrium. It must be remembered that it has been proved in Prop. VI. that in no case whatever can OE cut any horizontal line twice, nor can OG cut any vertical line twice. It is possible for OE in fig. 5, ultimately to bend back towards Oy, as does the dotted portion CD, if it happen that a very large amount of linen is incapable of being sold in England except on terms extremely advantageous to England.

The reader may exercise his fancy by drawing various forms which the curves may have consistently with the fundamental laws that have been laid down, and combining them in pairs so as to observe their possible points of intersection. After reading the next chapter he may interpret the points of intersection; of course the positions of the curves in fig. 5 are capable of being inverted. They would then represent a case in which the trade between the two countries could not grow up gradually; but could be carried on with profit to both if it were once started on a large scale by any external cause.

NOTE ON MILL'S TREATMENT OF AN EXCEPTIONAL CASE.

In § 6 of Ch. xviii. of Book III. Mill attempts to deal with difficulties in the theory of foreign trade, of which a solution is offered in the Examination of Class I. in the present Essay. He has seen that under certain circumstances there may be several different positions of equilibrium of trade : so that the problem arises of determining at which of these several positions the trade will remain. Mill has undertaken to illustrate by an example the method in which this general problem may be solved. But it appears to me that the special example which he has chosen does not illustrate the general problem in question. For I understand him to mean that the amount of cloth which England will expend on the purchase of linen is a given quantity, independent of the rate of interchange, say OV; and that the amount of linen which Germany is willing to expend in the purchase of cloth is a given quantity ; say OW. On this hypothesis the trade has only one possible position of equilibrium; viz. that in which OV cloth is exchanged for OW linen. Mill has proved, what indeed is obvious, that the division of the total benefits of the trade between the two countries depends upon the relative magnitudes of OV and OW.

Mill's example may be represented in a diagram thus. Draw (fig. 6) VPQ and WRS at right angles to Ox and Oy respectively, cutting one another in A. Let VP be the amount of linen which England could make for herself with the expense to which she is put in order to make and export OV cloth, then PQ is a portion of England's demand curve, which in this case has "degenerated" (in mathematical phrase) into a straight line. Similarly if WR be the amount of linen which Germany could make for herself with the expense to which she is put in order to make and export OW linen, then RS is a portion of Germany's demand curve. These two straight lines PQ and RS cannot intersect in more than one point. Mill's example therefore does not afford any aid towards the solution of the class of problems which are suggested by the intersections of the curves in figure 4. With regard to division of the benefits of the trade between the two countries it may be remarked that if A coincides with P England has to pay for her imported linen the full equivalent of what it would cost her to make it herself; and therefore she derives no benefit from the trade. So if A coincides with R, Germany derives no benefit from the trade. The further A is above P, the greater is the benefit that England derives from the trade: the further A is to the right of R, the greater is the benefit that Germany derives from the trade. Of course, by the conditions of the problem, A cannot lie below P, or to the left of R.

CHAPTER II.

STABLE AND UNSTABLE EQUILIBRIUM OF FOREIGN TRADE.

§ 1. IT will be convenient to have a name for the point Some technical terms are wanted. which corresponds to the actual position of the trade between England and Germany at any time. It generally happens in fact that the exports and imports of a country are not distributed evenly all over the year. Allowance must be made for these irregularities before the results of the pure theory can be applied to practice. But for the purposes of the pure theory it is allowable to assume that the importation and the consumption of foreign wares is distributed evenly all over the year.

Thus we may say that cloth is at any time being imported The scale of importation. into Germany on the scale of OM annually (or in a given unit of time); meaning thereby that the scale on which it is being imported is such that if it were to continue, the amount imported in the year (or unit of time) would be OM.

We have then the following:—

DEFINITION. If at any time cloth be exported from England Definition of Exchange-index. on the scale of OM annually, in exchange for linen on the scale of ON annually; and MP, NP be drawn at right angles to Ox, Oy respectively, meeting in P; then P is the exchange-index at that time.

It has been proved in Prop. IX. that the trade is in equilibrium when the exchange-index is at any point of intersection of OE and Oy. In the present chapter it will be shewn that some points of intersection correspond to stable equilibrium of the trade and others to unstable: and a fundamental law will be laid down by which the one set may be distinguished from the other. It will be convenient to commence by supposing that the exchange-index is not at A: but that some external disturbing force, as a war, or a bad harvest, has jerked the exchange-index to some position such that the trade corresponding to it is not in equilibrium; and to investigate the forces which will govern its motion.

We know from Prop. VI. that OE cannot cut a horizontal straight line through P more than once: and that OG cannot cut a vertical straight line through P more than once. We may have therefore the following

Definition of the phrases, "to the right of OE," "above OG."   DEFINITION. A point P is said to be *to the right* or *to the left* of OE according as it is to the right or the left of the point in which OE is cut by the horizontal straight line through P: and the point P is said to be *above* or *below* OG according as it is above or below the point in which OG is cut by a vertical straight line through P.

§ 2. The greater part of the pure theory of foreign trade consists of a series of corollaries from the laws with regard to the shapes of OE and OG, which were laid down in the last chapter, together with the following law :—

The law of the forces which control the movement of the Exchange-index.   PROP. XI. *If the Exchange-index be at any time to the right of* OE *it will tend to move to the left; if it be to the left of* OE *it will tend to move to the right. Similarly, if the Exchange-index be at any time above* OG *it will tend to move downwards; if it be below* OG *it will tend to move upwards.*

Such interpretation as this proposition may require will be contained in the proof of it. It must be remembered it is assumed throughout that the export trade of each country is conducted by private traders competing against one another. So that when the terms on which a country's foreign trade is conducted are such as to afford a rate of profits higher than the rate current in other industries, the competition of traders to obtain these higher profits will lead to an increase in the exportation of her wares : and *vice versa* when the rate of profits in the foreign trade are exceptionally low.

Let the exchange-point P be to the left of OE, as in fig. 7, and let NP produced cut OE in Q. Then since Q is a point on OE, ON linen is capable of being disposed of annually in England in exchange for the means of producing and exporting NQ cloth. But at the time in question linen is being imported on the scale of ON annually, and cloth is being exported in exchange for it on the scale of only NP annually. Consequently the exportation of cloth in exchange for linen must be a trade which affords abnormally high profits. Consequently, since competition in the trade is supposed to be free, the exportation of cloth will increase. Therefore when the exchange-index is to the left of OE it will tend to move to the right. So if the exchange-point lay at P' in NQ produced, it would shew that cloth was being exported at the rate of NP' annually in exchange for an amount of linen ON, which could be disposed of in England only for the expenses of producing and exporting NQ cloth : consequently the exportation of cloth would tend to diminish, *i.e.* when the exchange-point is to the right of OE, it will tend to move to the left.

Similar proofs apply to the second part of the proposition which relates to OG.

In order therefore to determine the directions in which the amounts of the exports of cloth and linen are tending to change at any time, it is requisite only to determine the position of the exchange-index at that time, and through it to draw arrowheads—an arrowhead pointing towards the right if the exchange-index lies on the left of OE, towards the left if this point lies on the right of OE; and an arrowhead pointing upwards if the exchange-index lies below OG, downwards if this point lies above OG[1].

The exchange-index will in each case tend to move in some direction within the angle made by the arrowheads. Thus, if the exchange-index be at P (fig. 7), it will tend to move in some direction lying within the angle RPQ. So that, unless some external event should arise to disturb the trade relations between the two countries, the exchange-index must soon strike either OE between Q and A, or OG between R and A. But, as we cannot tell the relative magnitude of the horizontal tendency along PQ, and of the vertical tendency along PR, we cannot predict which of the two curves it will strike first. Suppose it strike OE first: when it is on OE there will be no force tending to make it move either to the right or to the left. But there will be a force attracting it upwards. It will therefore tend to oscillate along QA towards A. For we may use this brief phrase to express the fact that the exchange-index will not necessarily remain on QA during the whole of its motion to A, but may oscillate first on one side of QA and then on the other: under the action of the forces which urge it to the right whenever it is to the left of OE, and to the left whenever it is to the right of OE. It will, however, unless its movements be disturbed by some powerful cause extraneous to the ordinary circumstances of the trade, in general adhere somewhat closely to QA. It will be convenient also

---

[1] Thus the motion of the exchange-index is in every respect similar to that of a material particle moving freely under the action of forces which attract it towards OE and OG. Suppose OE to be a rigid wire which exerts attractions only in a horizontal direction and always towards the right when the particle is, according to the definition in the text, on the left of OE, and vice versa. Similarly suppose OG to be a rigid wire which exerts attractions only in a vertical direction, and always upwards when the particle is, according to the definition in the text, below OG, and vice versa. Then this particle will move exactly in the same manner as does our exchange-index, so that if we chose to assign to these horizontal and vertical forces any particular laws, we should obtain a differential equation for the motion of the exchange-index. This equation when integrated would give us the path which on this particular supposition the particle would describe. Such calculations might afford considerable scope to the ingenuity of those who devise mathematical problems, but as we shall see further on (§ 6) they would afford no aid to the Economist.

to place at each of several points on the curve an arrowhead, to indicate the direction in which the exchange-index, if at that point, would be made to oscillate along the curve on which it is by the force exerted on it by the other curve. Similarly, if the exchange-index moving from P had struck the curve OG first, it would have oscillated along RA towards A.

Exactly in the same way it may be proved that if the exchange-index were at any time at P' it would be impelled by the forces acting on it to move upwards to the left : that if it struck OE first it would oscillate along QA towards A; and that if it struck OG first it would oscillate along GA towards A. And similarly for the points P'' and P'''.

Finally, if the exchange-index coming towards A shoot beside it or beyond it in any direction, or if the exchange-index be displaced by any disturbing event from A in any direction, the forces acting upon it will bring it back to OE or OG, and cause it to oscillate along that curve which it strikes first toward A.

§ 3. It will be convenient to speak of the equilibrium of the trade between England and Germany corresponding to a point of intersection of OE and OG as the equilibrium at that point. We may now give a formal

Definition of Stable and Unstable Equilibrium. DEFINITION. The equilibrium at a point of intersection of OE and OG is *stable*, provided that when the exchange-index strikes either of the curves in the neighbourhood of that point, the forces acting on the index tend to make it oscillate along the curve *towards* that point. In other cases the equilibrium is *unstable*.

It will be seen hereafter that the equilibrium at every point in which OE and OG cut one another, if it is unstable for displacements in any direction, is unstable for displacements in every direction. But this result does not hold of points in which the curves meet but touch without cutting one another.

We may now enunciate the fundamental rule for deciding whether any particular point of intersection of the curves corresponds to a stable or to an unstable equilibrium of the trade. But, in order that this may be given in a convenient form, it is necessary to have some handy means of distinguishing the various directions in which different parts of the curves may lie.

If a point moves from O along OE in fig. 8, it at first increases its distance from Oy at the same time that it increases its distance from Ox. It continues to do so until it arrives at R when the direction of the curve is vertical. If the point continues its motion from R onwards to C and B, it will continue to recede, but it will approach towards Oy. It will be

convenient to express the difference between the portions of
OE by saying that between O and R the curve is inclined
positively; and that from R to B, and for some distance beyond
B, the curve is inclined *negatively.*   Or more generally :—

Whatever portion of a curve lies in such a direction that
a point, which moves along it so as to recede from Ox, recedes
also from Oy; that portion of the curve is said to be *inclined
positively.*   Conversely, whatever portion of a curve lies in such
a direction that a point which moves along it so as to recede
from Ox approaches Oy; that portion of the curve is said to
be *inclined negatively.*

Using these terms we may enunciate

PROP. XII.   *The equilibrium is stable at every point of intersection of* OE *and* OG, *excepting those at which both curves are
inclined positively, but* OG *is more nearly vertical than* OE, *and
excepting those at which both curves are inclined negatively, but*
OG *is more nearly vertical than* OE.

In accordance with this Proposition, the equilibria at A
and C in each of the figures 8 and 9 (which are repetitions of
figs. 4 and 5 respectively) are stable, and the equilibrium at
B in each of these figures is unstable, as has been already
indicated.   The most convenient mode of establishing this
Proposition is perhaps to draw a number of figures repre-
sentative of every position in which the curves can lie at a
point of intersection.   Arrowheads should then be inserted to
indicate, in conformity with Prop. XI., the directions of the
forces which would act upon the exchange-index at different
points in the figures, so as to exhibit the motion of the exchange-index.

If through B in fig. 8 there be drawn the straight lines
TBU from left to right, and VBW vertically upwards, then,
if the exchange-point be displaced to a position within the
quadrant TBW, it will tend to move to A.   If displaced to a
position within the quadrant VBU it will tend to move to C.
If displaced to a position in either of the quadrants TBV,
WBU, it will tend to move to A or C, according to whether
the forces acting upon it bring it into the quadrant TBW, or
into the quadrant VBU.   In this last case it is just possible
that the exchange-index may on its way back strike B.   This
possibility is worthy of note.   But the motion of the exchange-
index is not likely to be arrested at B; and if disturbed from
B ever so little along either of the curves it would tend to
move off to A or C.   Therefore it is not inaccurate to describe
the equilibrium at B as unstable.   Indeed precisely analogous
cases occur in Mechanics.   A body displaced from equilibrium
may pass through a position of unstable equilibrium on its way

towards a position of stable equilibrium. Similar remarks apply to the unstable equilibrium at B in fig. 9.

The informal proof of the proposition that has already been suggested might perhaps suffice. But it seems advisable to indicate the manner in which a formal proof of it may be given.

Let then D be any point of intersection of OE and OG. Let horizontal and vertical straight lines TDU, VDW be drawn as in fig. 10.

Firstly let England's curve be inclined positively at D: let it point at D in the direction of the straight line eDE. Then will the equilibrium be stable provided that at D Germany's curve either (i) be inclined positively but make a greater angle with the vertical than eDE does, pointing at D for instance in the direction of gDG; or (ii) be inclined negatively, and pointing at D for instance in the direction of $g'DG'$: or in other words provided that Germany's curve lie within the angles eDW, EDV.

For suppose the exchange-index to strike OE just below D, then it must be below OG, whether OG lie in the direction gD or $g'D$; because eD lies below both gD and $g'D$: therefore it must be attracted upwards. Therefore the arrowhead on eD must point towards D. So it may be proved that the arrowhead on DE points towards D: and that the arrowheads on gD and DG, and on $g'D$ and DG' all point towards D. Which proves that under the stated condition D is a point of stable equilibrium.

In exactly the same manner it may be proved that the equilibrium at D will be unstable if while England's curve lies at D in the direction eDE Germany's curve is positively inclined and makes a smaller angle with the vertical than eDE does, and lies therefore in the angles eDV, WDE.

In the same manner also it may be proved that if OE is inclined negatively at D, the equilibrium at D is stable unless OG be inclined negatively at D and be more nearly vertical than OE is, which completes the proof of the Proposition.

§ 4. It may promote clear conceptions with regard to the drift of the above reasoning if some portion of it be expressed directly in terms of the motives which govern the exportation of cloth and of linen. Let us take for this purpose the case in which the exchange-index has been jerked by some disturbance from OC to the point P in fig. 8 within the loop BC. This may mean that some abnormal event such for instance as a passing difficulty in the English cloth producing trade, has checked the supply of cloth, so that cloth is imported into Germany on the scale of OM yards annually instead of OL annually. Although Germany would be willing permanently to purchase this amount only by giving linen in return for it on the scale of QM yards annually; yet being taken by surprise, and unprovided with a substitute for cloth, or for some other transitional cause she pays for it on the scale of PM yards of linen annually. Let us then inquire what tendencies there will be, as soon as the disturbance is past, to increase or diminish the scales on which cloth and linen are sent from one country to the other.

Let us look first at Germany's side of the case. As soon as the disturbing causes have ceased to operate, cloth imported on the scale of OM yards annually will be capable of being disposed of in Germany only on terms so disadvantageous to England as not to enable linen to be exported in exchange for it on a scale as great as that of PM annually. Consequently those who export linen from Germany will find it unprofitable to carry on an extensive trade until they are able to obtain cloth on more favourable terms of interchange. Therefore there will be a diminution in the scale on which linen is exported from Germany.

England's side of the case is the reverse of this. Linen imported on the scale of PM annually will be capable of being disposed of in England on terms which will enable cloth to be exported in exchange for it on the scale of more than OM annually. Consequently the exporters of cloth from England will find that their trade affords at the present rates of interchange abnormally high profits. These traders are supposed to act not in combination, but in free competition with one another; so that each of them will strive to obtain for himself as large a share as possible of this profitable trade and will push the sale of his cloth to Germany even if in order to do so he should be compelled to submit to a slight reduction of the price on which he disposes of it. Therefore there will be an increase in the scale on which cloth is exported from England. That is to say the exchange-index will move from P downwards to the right until it strikes OE or OG. Suppose it to strike OG first in the point F. At this time cloth is being imported from England on the scale of OZ annually, and linen exported in exchange for it on the scale of FZ annually: and with this state of the trade Germany is just satisfied. The terms on which cloth can be sold in Germany are just sufficient to sustain the trade in this position. But linen imported into England on the scale of FZ annually can be disposed of there on terms more than sufficiently advantageous to cover the expenses of exporting cloth on the scale of OZ annually: consequently the exportation of cloth will continue to increase. So long as the exchange-index remains on OG the only force tending to change its motion will be a horizontal force to the right. But if the index falls below OG the exporters of linen from Germany will have an inducement to extend their sales to England; and *vice versa* if the index rises above OG they will at once contract their sales to England. Whereby the index will be compelled to oscillate along OG towards C. So if the index had struck OE first, it would have been compelled to oscillate along OE towards C. Therefore the equilibrium at C is stable.

In the course of the proof of Prop. XII. it was proved implicitly that if at a point of intersection of the two curves, the equilibrium was stable for displacements in any one direction it was stable for displacements in all directions: and similarly for unstable equilibrium. Of course these results are capable of an easy independent proof.

But if the curves touch without cutting one another, those arrowheads on the curves which are on one side of the point of contact will be directed towards that point and those which are on the other will be directed away from it as in figure 11. In fact the position of OE in this figure is obtained from the position which it has in fig. 8 by pressing it downwards so that the two points of intersection B and C in fig. 8 run together to make the point of contact D in fig. 11. So that D is really two coincident points of intersection one of which corresponds to stable and the other to unstable equilibrium.

Of course, since disturbances of equilibrium occur in every direction, a point at which equilibrium is unstable for displacements in any direction is a point at which trade cannot rest and therefore has no practical importance. An investigation of the many various conditions under which the curves may touch one another will afford to the reader some curious amusement; but so far as at present appears, it is devoid of any practical utility.

§ 5. PROP. XIII. *If from a point of intersection of* OE *and* OG *at which the equilibrium is stable we proceed along either of the curves in either direction until we arrive at another point of intersection, this second point must be one of unstable equilibrium, and vice versa.*

This proposition is obviously true. For if we proceed from a point of intersection along that portion of OE which lies above OG; and place arrowheads on OE on our way, these must all point downwards until we come up to the next point of intersection, therefore that point of intersection is unstable. And a precisely similar proof applies, mutatis mutandis, to every other case. It may be an interesting exercise to attempt to draw diagrams in which one of the curves shall be represented as passing through two points of stable equilibrium consecutively, or through two points of unstable equilibrium; and to notice how each attempt is foiled by the necessity of conforming to the fundamental laws of the curves. Of course the Proposition is capable of a direct geometrical proof.

It was proved in Prop. V. that if OE belong to the Normal Class or Class I., that portion of OE which is adjacent to O lies below that portion of OG which is adjacent to O. Therefore arrowheads placed on OE in the neighbourhood of O must point upwards and those placed on OG must point to the right. Therefore the first point of intersection at which we arrive if we proceed along either of the curves from O must be a point of stable equilibrium. In other words, O is a point of unstable equilibrium if both the curves belong to the Normal Class or to Class I. But if either of them belong to Class II. O may be a point of stable equilibrium, and the first point of intersection at which we arrive when we pass along either of the curves from O may be a point of unstable equilibrium.

In this last case the total number of points of intersection (O not being included,) will be two or some other even number. But in every other case the total number must be one or three, or some other odd number. For it is obvious that if we proceed from O along either of the curves, the last point of intersection that we arrive at must be one of stable equilibrium.

§ 6. We have seen how the position of the exchange-index relatively to OE and OG determines the directions of the horizontal and of the vertical force which act on it: but there are no general laws by which the magnitude of each of these forces can be determined. Therefore even if we knew exactly the shapes which the curves assumed in any particular problem, we should not have data on which to base a calculation of the precise path which the exchange point would describe [1].

The task of discovering laws by which the shapes of the curves may in any case be approximately determined does not appear to transcend the resources which the science of statistics at present affords us. It will indeed, be a long time before this task is achieved: when it is achieved, it may be worth while to

---

[1] For the mathematical functions introduced into the original differential equation could not, in the present condition of our knowledge, be chosen so as to represent even approximately the economic forces that actually operate in the world. And by integrating them we should move further away from, instead of approaching nearer to the actual facts of life. For this reason, among others, the method of diagrams seems to me to be generally speaking of greater use to the Economist, than the methods of mathematical analysis. For when using the former method we have continually before us those assumptions which are justified by economic facts, and no others. Whereas the use of mathematical analysis has been found to tempt men to expend their energy on the elaboration of minute and complex hypotheses, which have indeed some distant analogy to economic conditions, but which cannot properly be said to represent in any way economic laws.

hand over the curves to be manipulated by the processes of analytical mathematics: but until then, the mathematical treatment of the curve cannot lead us to any results which cannot be at once obtained from inspection of the diagrams. Even then the methods of mathematical analysis will not be able to afford any considerable assistance in the task of determining the motion of the exchange-index. For a large amount of additional work will have to be done before we can obtain approximate laws for representing the magnitude of the horizontal and vertical forces which will act upon the exchange-index in any position.

Finally, even when this is done there will yet remain a further difficulty in the way of the mathematical treatment of the problem. It is necessary to inquire with considerable care into this difficulty ; because it extends so far as even to impair to some extent the efficiency of the treatment of the problem by the method of diagrams.

§ 7. It has been remarked, that in economics every event causes permanent alterations in the conditions under which future events can occur. This is to some extent; the case in the physical world, but not to nearly so great an extent. The forces that act on a pendulum in any position are not to any appreciable extent dependent on the oscillations that the pendulum has already made. And there are many other classes of movement in the physical world, which are exact copies of movements that have gone before. But every movement that takes place in the moral world alters the magnitude if not the character of the forces that govern succeeding movements. And economic forces belong to the moral world in so far as they depend upon human habits and affections, upon man's knowledge and industrial skill. Where, for instance, any casual disturbance increases the amount of English wares of any kind that are consumed in Germany it leaves behind it a permanent effect in an increased familiarity on the part of German consumers with English wares; and in this and other ways occasions permanent alterations in the circumstances of demand. An alteration of the shape of Germany's demand curve is rendered necessary by any change which alters the amount of German wares that can be exported annually with the proceeds of the sale in Germany of any given amount of English wares. Consequently, every movement of the exchange-index entails some alteration in the shapes of the curves, and therefore in the forces which determine its succeeding movements. If the curves belong to the Normal Class, or to Class I., the alterations thus required are not likely to be extensive. At all events, the general character of the curves will seldom be changed : and though the positions of equilibrium may be slightly shifted; the general tenor of the reasonings that have been based on the assumption that the shapes of the curves remain rigid and unchanged, will not be thereby invalidated.

But these reasonings may be frequently invalidated if either of the curves belongs to Class II. For suppose that an increase in the amount of cloth produced for exportation leads to the introduction of extensive economies. Such economies when they have once been obtained are not readily lost. Developments of mechanical appliances, of division of labour, and of organisation of transport, when they have once been effected are not readily abandoned. Capital and skilled labour which have once been devoted to any particular industry, may indeed become depreciated in value when there is a falling off in the demand for the wares which they produce; but they cannot quickly be converted to other occupations. So that for a time their competition will prevent a diminished demand from causing an increased price of the wares.

Thus for instance the shape of OE in fig. 12 implies that if cloth were produced for exportation on the scale of OU annually, the economies introduced into its production would be so extensive as to enable it to be produced and exported for a total price which would be covered by the sale in England of linen on the scale of TU annually. If these economies were once effected the shape of the curve would probably cease to represent accurately the circumstances of England's demand. The expenses of production, for instance, of OV cloth would no longer be much greater proportionately than those of OU cloth: so that cloth on the scale of OV annually could be produced and exported by means of the proceeds of the sale of linen imported on a scale considerably less than that of RV. Thus in order that the curve might again represent the circumstances of England's demand it would be necessary to draw it lower down; possibly so much lower as to make it fall in the position of the dotted curve in the figure, so as to have only one point of intersection with OG. And generally if the circumstances of the production of cloth are such that an increased production of it for exportation, within certain limits, cause greatly increased economies in its production; then the curve between these limits will require some special treatment. For it can be taken to represent the conditions of England's demand only before and up to the occurrence of any event which renders it profitable to produce cloth on a large scale for a time sufficiently long for the introduction of these economies. After the occurrence of such an event, the curve must be, partially at least, re-drawn. Thus if at a point just to the right of this portion of the curve there be drawn, in accordance with the rules laid down, an arrowhead pointing to the left; this arrowhead will indicate a resistance that must be overcome before the exchange-index can move to this point. But if by any means the exchange-index is brought to this point, the existence of the arrowhead will not justify us in assuming without investigation that in the corresponding practical problem there will be in operation a force tending to make the exchange-index move toward the left. Conclusions based upon the assumption of the rigidity of the curves may be applied to practical problems coming under Class II. in so far as the conclusions relate to the resistances which must be overcome before there can be effected an increase in the scale on which cloth or linen is exported: but not in so far as they relate to the forces which may operate to diminish this scale. Therefore the account of positions of unstable equilibrium which has been deduced from an examination of the curves in Class II. may not be applied to practical problems generally until a careful inquiry has been instituted in each particular case as to the probability that economies which had once been introduced, would be quickly lost. It is chiefly for this reason that as has already been said the results obtained from the curves in Class II. are of less importance than those obtained in the Normal Class and in Class I. But though they cannot so far as at present appears be largely used for the immediate deduction of conclusions in matters of practice, there seems to be large scope for the use of them in the suggestion of new practical problems.

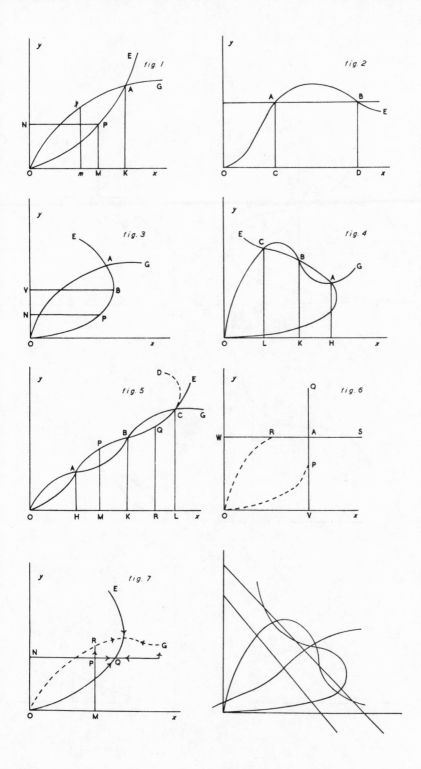

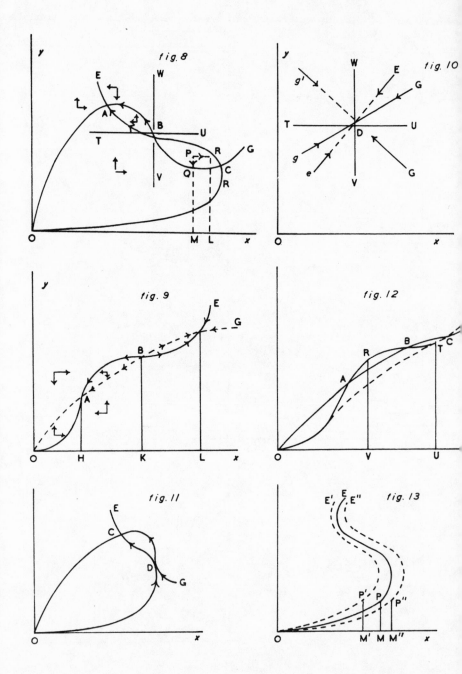

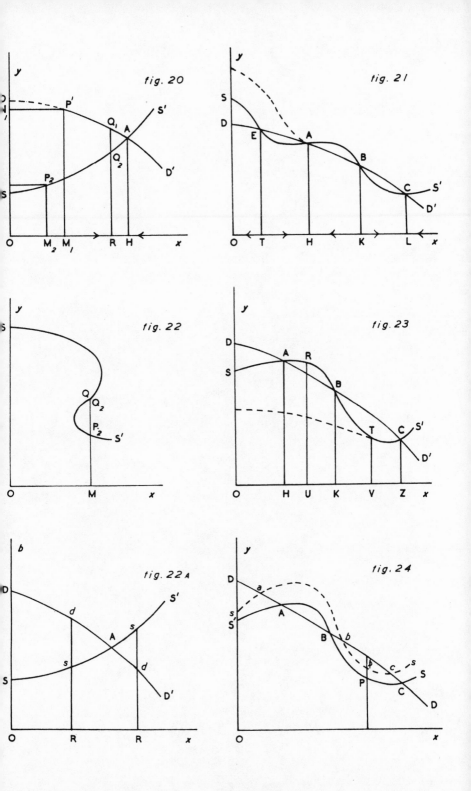

THE

PURE THEORY OF (DOMESTIC) VALUES.

CHAPTER I.

§ 1. In the present part of the treatise we are concerned with the causes which determine the relative values of commodities produced in the same country under the action of free competition. This theory is called by Mill and others the "theory of Value," but I prefer to call it "the theory of Domestic values." For the term "theory of value" is a generic term, and ought, I think, to be interpreted so as to include the theory of Domestic values and the theory of International values. The apparatus of diagrams which was best adapted for the investigation of the latter will not be of service here; where another apparatus must accordingly be supplied.

The necessity of this change can be easily seen. For in the theory of international values it is important to bring out the similarity between the positions in which the country that buys and the country that sells any particular ware stand to one another. And, to refer to the example of foreign trade which was discussed in the previous Part, the economic causes that govern Germany's willingness to exchange her linen for English cloth are in every respect homogeneous with those that govern England's willingness to exchange her cloth for German linen. It was expedient, therefore, that the curves which represented the respective demands of England and Germany should be drawn on the same principle. This would not have been effected if we had taken distances along Ox to represent numbers of yards of cloth, and distances measured along Oy to represent the exchange value of cloth in terms of linen. Such an arrangement of the diagrams would have some advantages; but it would have involved the laying down of two complete sets of laws for the construction of the curves; so that, in fact, the laws which governed the shape of Germany's curve would have been in no respect similar to or symmetrical with those which governed the shape of England's curve. This want of symmetry would have marred, though it would not have rendered impracticable, the application of the method of diagrams to the more elementary portions of the theory ; but in other portions it would have led to unmanageable complications.

In the theory of Domestic values on the other hand, the causes that determine the price at which producers are willing to bring into the market any given amount of a commodity are, in most respects, of a different character from the causes which determine the price at which consumers are willing to buy any given amount. There is not in the nature of the case any symmetry between these two sets of causes. Therefore it is useless to attempt to express the operation of these two sets of causes by curves, the laws of which shall be symmetrical.

It may at first sight seem that in consequence of the absence of symmetry the diagrams which interpret the pure theory of Domestic values must be very complex. But it is not so; for this theory, although in one respect it is at a disadvantage relatively to the pure theory of International values, yet has a compensating advantage. In the theory of Domestic values it is not necessary to consider at one time the special circumstances of more than one commodity; whereas in the theory of International values, with the partial exception of a certain portion of it, to be discussed hereafter, it is necessary to consider together the circumstances that govern the demand for at least two commodities, as e.g. cloth and linen. The importance of this advantage is so great that the application of the method of diagrams to the former theory involves on the whole less difficulty than does its application to the latter theory.

§ 2. The progress of the theory of Domestic values has been much hindered by contentions as to the relation in which value stands to "cost of production," and the meaning which is to be attributed to this phrase. The phrase is used in two different senses. Sometimes it means the sum total of the efforts and abstinences which have been undergone by the various labourers and capitalists who have had share in the production. At other times it means the economic measure of these efforts and abstinences, i.e. the price that must be paid by any person who wishes to purchase them.

In the present investigation we are concerned with cost of production only in its latter use, or, as I prefer saying, with "expenses of production." We have to deal only with the machinery of exchange. We have not to estimate the fatigue

or discomfort which must be undergone by those who perform
any given task; we have only to consider the price which must
be paid to them in order to induce them to perform it. We
have to consider the consequences which result from the great
central law of economic science.

This law is that "producers, each governed under the sway
of free competition by calculations of his own interest, will
endeavour so to regulate the amount of any commodity which
is produced for a given market during a given period, that this
amount shall be just capable on the average of finding purchasers during this period at a remunerative price. A remunerative price is to be interpreted to be a price which shall be
just equal to the sum of the exchange or economic measures of
those efforts and sacrifices which are required for the production
of the commodity when the amount in question is produced.
These economic measures are the expenses which must be in-
curred by a person who would purchase the performance of these
efforts and sacrifices[1]."

Accordingly, we take as before two fixed straight lines Ox and
Oy at right angles to one another. But while we take distances
along Ox to represent amounts of the commodity in question, we
must take distances measured along Oy to represent values of a
unit of the commodity; as e.g. a ton, if the commodity be coal;
a yard, if the commodity be cloth, &c. These values must be
measured in terms of some other commodity; in general it is
convenient to measure them in terms of money, or, which is the
same thing, in terms of command over commodities in general,
so that distances measured along Oy represent prices. The
curves are capable of being applied in the solution of many
problems concerning market values. But here they will be
applied only to average values.

§ 3. Let us consider first the curve which represents the
circumstances of the average demand in a given market for a
particular commodity; say for coal, supposed to be all of uni-
form quality. The market may be a district of any size; it
may be the whole of a country. The amount of coals which
will be bought or "demanded" in a given time, say in a year, will
depend upon the average price at which they are offered for
sale. Thus, if it is possible to dispose of, say, a million tons
annually in this market, at an average price of 25s. a ton; it
would not have been possible to dispose of eleven hundred
thousand tons annually, save at a lower price, say at an average
of 23s. a ton. Let us suppose that we know the price at which
each several amount of coals can be disposed of annually. If

[1] From an article by the present writer in the *Fortnightly Review* for April,
1876.

then we measure numbers of tons of coals along Ox and the number of shillings in the price of a ton of coals along Oy, we may draw what may be called "the Demand curve," thus : Let M be any point on Ox (fig. 20), and let the price at which it is possible to dispose of OM_1 coals annually be estimated and found to be equal to ON_1. Draw M_1P_1 and N_1P_1 at right angles to Ox and Oy respectively to meet in P_1. Then P_1 is a point on the curve. By causing M_1 to move continuously from O along Ox, and finding the position of P_1 corresponding to each position of M_1, we can obtain a continuous series of positions for P_1; i.e. we can make P_1 describe the curve which we are seeking.

Of course it may not be possible to conjecture, with any approach to accuracy, the price at which it would be possible to dispose of a quantity of the commodity, either very much greater or very much less than that amount which is wanted to be sold in the market in question. Consequently in the discussion of any particular practical problem the demand curve can be regarded as trustworthy, only within somewhat narrow limits on either side of this amount. But this difficulty is of importance only in connexion with Applied Economics. In Pure Economics, with which alone we are concerned here, we may suppose the curve to be properly drawn throughout its whole length.

Recollecting that P_1M_1 is equal to ON_1 we may define the Demand curve thus:

The Demand curve DD_1 for a commodity in a market is such that if any point P_1 be taken on it, and P_1M_1 be drawn perpendicular to Ox, P_1M_1 represents the price per unit, at which an amount of the commodity, represented by OM_1, is capable of being sold in the market in each year (or other given period).

Since every increase in OM_1 causes a decrease in PM_1, a point moving from D along DD_1 will continually increase its distance from Oy and diminish its distance from Ox. We may here recall a definition already given. It has been said :

Whatever portion of a curve lies in such a direction that a point which moves along it so as to recede from Ox recedes also from Oy; that portion of the curve is said to be *inclined positively*. Conversely, whatever portion of a curve lies in such a direction that a point which moves along it so as to recede from Ox approaches Oy; that portion of the curve is said to be *inclined negatively*.

With this definition we may enunciate

PROP. XVII. *The Demand Curve is throughout inclined negatively.*

§ 4. On similar principles we may draw the curve which

represents the circumstances of the average supply of the commodity: or as we may say, "the Supply Curve." It may be
that every increase in the amount supplied involves a more
than proportional increase in the expense of producing it. Thus
we may suppose that if a million tons annually can be raised
and brought into the market at a price of 25s. a ton, the requisite allowance being made for traders' profits of various kinds;
that for an annual supply of nine hundred thousand tons, a
price of 23s. would be sufficient; but that for an annual supply
of eleven hundred thousand tons, a price of 27s. would be required. Let us suppose that we know the price which is sufficient to cover the expenses of production of each several
amount of coal supplied annually in the market. We may then
draw the Supply curve thus:

Let M_2 be any point on Ox, fig. 20. Let the price which
will just cover the expenses of producing and bringing into the
market OM_2 tons of coal annually be calculated and found equal
to ON_2. Draw M_2P_2, and N_2P_2, at right angles to Ox and Oy
respectively to meet in P_2. Then P_2 is a point on the curve. By
causing M_2 to move continuously from O along Ox, and finding
the position of P_2 corresponding to each position of M_2, we can
obtain a continuous series of positions for P_2: i. e. we can make
P_2 describe the curve which we are seeking.

The calculations necessary for drawing the Supply curve in
any particular practical problem, are in general trustworthy
only for amounts either very much greater or very much less
than that which is wanted actually to be sold in the market in
question. But as has been already remarked with reference to
the Demand curve, this difficulty does not prevent us from reasoning in pure Economics on the supposition that the curve
is properly drawn throughout its whole length.

We may then define the Supply curve thus:

The Supply curve SS' for a commodity in a market is such
that if any point P_2 be taken on it, and P_2M_2 drawn perpendicular to Ox, P_2M_2 represents the price per unit at which a supply of the commodity of which the amount is represented by
OM_2 can be remuneratively produced and brought into the
market in each year (or other given period).

The law which governs the shape of this curve is not so
simple as the corresponding law for the Demand curve. Some
remarks will be made in the following section as to the manner in
which an increase in the total production of any commodity affects the price at which its producers can afford to offer it for sale.
For the present we may assume that in general an increase in the
production of a raw commodity can be effected only at a more
than proportionately increased expense: while an increase in

the demand for manufactured commodities in most cases tends to a diminution of the price at which they can be offered for sale. Thus if SS' be the Supply curve for a raw commodity, the law in most but not in all cases will be, that if a point moves from S along the curve it will increase its distance from Ox at the same time that it increases its distance from Oy: or in other words, that the curve is inclined positively throughout. If, however, SS' be the Supply curve for a manufactured commodity, the law in most, but not in all, cases will be that if a point moves from S along the curve, it will while increasing its distance from Oy diminish its distance from Ox. But after the point has moved in this way for a certain distance, it may cease to approach Ox, and begin to recede from it. For it may happen that a further increase in the amount produced will not render possible any important further economies in the production; and that in consequence of the increasing expense to which manufacturers are put in obtaining additional supplies of the raw material or of labour, any further increase in the amount produced can be profitably effected only at an increased price. But again, the production of an amount considerably larger than this may render possible further economies of such magnitude as to outweigh the tendency which the expense of obtaining additional supplies of labour and of raw material has to increase the price at which the commodity can be produced. So that as the point continues to move along SS' it may, while continuing to recede from Oy, again commence to approach Ox, and so on. Thus SS' may have the shape that is given to it in fig. 21. This result may be expressed by saying that it is possible that some portions of the supply curve may be positively inclined and others negatively. It is, however, obvious that the Supply curve cannot bend backwards after the manner of the curve drawn in fig. 22. For the circumstances on which the difficulty of production of any given amount OM_2 of the commodity depends, being definite; it cannot be true that each of two prices P_2M_2 and QM_2 is just sufficient to render remunerative the production of the same amount OM_2. Hence we obtain the only law to which the Supply curve must in all cases conform, viz.:

PROP. XVIII. *The Supply Curve cannot cut twice any vertical straight line.*

It may be observed that the law that has been given with regard to the shape of the Demand curve includes the law:

The Demand curve cannot cut twice either any vertical straight line or any horizontal straight line.

The extent to which § 5. No attempt can be made in the present work fully to investigate the data which would be required for the construction of the supply curve in any particular case. For in such an attempt it would be necessary to work over a very large portion of the ground covered by the science of applied Economics. Enough has been said to indicate to those who are already acquainted with that science the general character of the required investigation[1]. But I would venture to remark that the customary method of treating the advantages of division of labour and of production on a large scale appears to me to be in one respect defective. For the manner in which these advantages are discussed in most Economic treatises is such as to imply that the most important of them can as a rule be obtained only by the concentration of large masses of workmen in vast establishments. If this were the rule, it would be reasonable to object that the introduction of economies into the process of manufacture does not depend directly and in the main on the magnitude of the total amount of the commodity produced. It may indeed be argued that an industry which gives employment to only some twenty thousand men altogether may happen to be concentrated in the hands of a few large firms, and may thus have command over most of the more important advantages of production on a large scale. And it may be argued that industries of far larger dimensions may be conducted almost entirely by small masters. Such, for instance, is the case with some of the metal trades and with the trades of boot-making and tailoring in England. The answer to this objection is twofold.

In the first place it must be insisted that such industries as the two last mentioned are not fairly to be classed as manufacturing industries. For in them the producer who is brought into immediate contact with the consumer is generally in a position of great advantage relatively to the manufacturer, who lives at a distance from the ultimate purchaser of his wares, and who has to make them to fit a number of lay models. But even in trades of this class, when the progress of invention renders possible important economies of which none but large establishments can avail themselves, such establishments will rise more speedily and more surely if the total demand for the produce of the industry is great than if it is small. I may quote, in illustration of this principle, the history of the boot-making trade in America: in which the growth of large establishments and a localized industry has been simultaneous with the development of various forms of the sewing machine and of other great economies in manufacture. And the clothing trades in America and elsewhere appear to be entering upon a similar phase.

We may then properly limit the title of manufacturing

the economies derived from manufacturing on a large scale depend on the amount of the total production.

Characteristics of industries

---

[1] But compare the Appendix on Mill's *Theory of Value.*

which may industries to those the produce of which is adapted for being
properly dealt with wholesale, which do not require the producer to be
be called brought into immediate contact with the consumer; which are
manufac- not concerned with raising raw produce from the earth; and
turing. which give scope for various forms of specialised skill and
specialised machinery.

The term manufacturing industries when thus limited will
include the metal trades which have been referred to as being
mainly in the hands of small masters. This brings us to the
second portion of the answer to the objection with which we are
dealing. For in these trades the advantages of production on a
large scale can in general be as well attained by the aggregation
of a large number of small masters into one district as by the
erection of a few large works. It is true that the disadvantages
under which the small masters lie in the competition with large
firms are increasing more rapidly than are their peculiar advantages; and that in most though not in all directions there
is a tendency for small masters to be supplanted. But in the
metal trades in question, and in many others, the advantages
which are generally classed under the heads of division of labour
and production on a large scale can be attained almost as fully
by the aggregation into one district of many establishments of
a moderate size as by the erection of a few huge factories. The
customary method of treating the advantages of division of
labour appears to me to be defective, inasmuch as it takes but
little account of this fact. I cannot, however, do more here than
indicate in outline an explanation of it.

The ad-   Firstly, with regard to many classes of commodities it is
vantages possible to divide the process of production into several
which a   stages, each of which can be performed with the maximum of
large in- economy in a small establishment: though the larger capitalists
dustry,   have even in these cases superior advantages as regards the
particular- buying of materials, and occasionally as regards the selling of
ly if it be that which they produce. If there exist a large number of
localized, such small establishments specialised for the performance of a
may have particular stage of the process of production, there will be room
even if it for the profitable investment of capital in the organising of
be not   subsidiary industries adapted for meeting their special wants.
conducted The most important of these subsidiary industries fall chiefly
in large into two groups.
establish-
ments.

Subsidiary   One of these groups is occupied with making the special
industries. tools and machinery required for this stage of the production.
Such a task offers large scope for enterprise both in other ways
and in particular in the invention and erection of machinery
designed for making these special tools and machinery. But in
order that such a task may be efficiently performed, it is neces-

sary that the total demand for these tools and machinery should be very great.

The other group of subsidiary industries is occupied with collecting and distributing the various materials and other commodities which are required by the small establishments in question, and with collecting and distributing the produce of their work. This task will be performed partly by carriers, including those who make and manage railways and canals: partly by intermediate traders, some on a small scale and some on a large. In this class of subsidiary industries are to be reckoned also the trade newspaper and other agencies for collecting and disseminating information relating to particular trades.

Secondly, among the most important of the economies which are available in the production of many classes of commodities are those which are concerned with the education of specialised skill. When large masses of men in the same locality are engaged in similar tasks, it is found that, by associating with one another, they educate one another. To use a mode of speaking which workmen themselves use, the skill required for their work "is in the air, and children breathe it as they grow up." Moreover, a man who has the faculties required for the work of a foreman, or for any specially difficult class of manual work, is likely soon to be put to the best work for which he is fitted, if there are in his neighbourhood many workshops in which he may seek a berth. Thus nascent talent is quickly and surely developed. Again, the large extent of the market in which employers can seek skilled labour makes it easy for them, when they want to extend their business, to obtain additional supplies of ready trained workmen. And they escape that disorganisation of their business, which would arise if they could not easily fill up the gap occasioned by the illness or death of a foreman or other highly skilled workman.

The education and economy of technical skill.

Thirdly, if the total number of firms engaged in a particular industry is small, there are but few men in a position to make improvements in the processes of manufacture, to invent new machines and new methods. But when the total number of men interested in the matter is very large there are to be found among them many who, by their intellect and temper, are fitted to originate new ideas. Each new idea is canvassed and improved upon by many minds; each new accidental experience and each deliberate experiment will afford food for reflection and for new suggestions, not to a few persons but to many. Thus in a large localised industry new ideas are likely to be started rapidly: and each new idea is likely to be fertile of practical improvements.

The intercommunication of ideas.

This inter-communication of ideas has in recent times been rendered possible to a considerable extent, even in trades that are not localised, by the trade newspapers, to which reference has already been made. But such a newspaper cannot have an adequate supply of able editors and correspondents unless the trade interests with which it deals are on a sufficiently great scale to enable it to obtain a large circulation.

It may then be concluded that an increase in the total amount of a commodity manufactured can scarcely fail to occasion increased economies in the production, whether the task of production is distributed among a large number of small capitalists, or is concentrated in the hands of a comparatively small number of large firms.

§ 6. We shall want to represent geometrically the scale on which the total production of the commodity in question is being actually carried on at any particular time. For this purpose we have the following

DEFINITION. R (fig. 22 A) being a point on Ox, let OR measure the amount of the commodity which would be produced in a year if the scale on which the production is carried on at a given time were continued uniformly. Then R is the *Amount-index* at that time[1].

With this definition we may enunciate the fundamental

PROP. XIX. *Let a vertical straight line drawn through the Amount-index cut the Demand curve in* d, *and the Supply curve in* s. *If* d *is above* s *the Amount-index will tend to move to the right. If* d *is below* s *the Amount-index will tend to move to the left. If* d *coincides with* s, *as at* A, *the Amount-index will be in equilibrium, tending to move neither to the right nor to the left.*

For, R being the Amount-index, an amount OR can be produced just at the price Rs, and can be disposed of at the price Rd. If then Rd is greater than Rs, the producers will make at an expense Rs what they can sell at the price Rd; and will thus obtain over and above the ordinary profits on their capital a profit sd on each unit of the commodity they produce. The trade will therefore be exceptionally profitable, and capital will flow into it. Thus an increased amount of the commodity will be produced; or in other words, the Amount-index will move to the right. Again, if Rd, the price at which the amount OR can be disposed of annually in the market, be less than Rs, the price which is required to enable the business to return the ordinary profits to the capitalist, capital will leave the trade. Thus the production of the commodity will be diminished;

---

[1] Compare the definition of the term "Exchange-index" and the remarks on it in the *Pure Theory of Foreign Trade*, c. i. § 9.

that is, the Amount-index will move to the left. But if Rd be equal to Rs, the trade will return the ordinary profits to the capitalist; and there will be no tendency for the Amount-index to move either to the right or to the left. Of course Rd is equal to Rs when R is vertically below a point of intersection of the Demand and Supply curves. We may then formulate

PROP. XX. *The Amount-index is in equilibrium whenever it is vertically below any point of intersection of the Demand and Supply curves.*

It follows from Prop. XIX. that if in fig. 20 the Amount-index be anywhere between O and H it will tend to move to the right; if anywhere beyond H it will tend to move to the left. So in fig. 21 if the Amount-index be between O and T it will tend to move to the left; if between T and H, to the right; if between H and K, to the left; if between K and L, to the right; if beyond L, to the left. These results are indicated in each figure by arrowheads placed along Ox. They may be expressed by saying that A in fig. 20 and A and C in fig. 21 are points of stable equilibrium. But E and B in fig. 21 are points of unstable. For we may give the following

DEFINITION. If the Amount-index on being slightly displaced from any position in which it is at equilibrium tends to return to that position, the equilibrium is said to be *stable :* if not, it is said to be *unstable.* Thus, as an immediate consequence from Prop. XIV., we obtain

PROP. XXI. *The equilibrium of the Amount-index corresponding to any point of intersection of the Demand and Supply curves is stable or unstable according as the Demand curve lies above or below the Supply curve just to the left of that point.*

If the curves touch one another at any point, the equilibrium corresponding to it will be stable for displacements in one direction, and unstable for displacements in the other. No practical interest attaches to the investigation of this case[1].

It is obvious that if we move along either of the curves in either direction from one point of stable equilibrium to the next, we must pass through a point of unstable equilibrium. In other words, in cases in which the curves cut each other more than once points of stable and unstable equilibrium alternate.

Also the last point of intersection reached as we move to the right must be a point of stable equilibrium. For if the amount produced were increased indefinitely the price at which it could be sold would necessarily fall almost to zero: but the

---

[1] Compare the remarks on the analogous case, *Pure Theory of Foreign Trade,* c. II. § 4.

price required to cover its expenses of production would not so fall. Therefore if a point moves to the right along the Supply curve it must ultimately rise and remain above the Demand curve.

The first point of intersection arrived at as we proceed from left to right may be a point either of stable or of unstable equilibrium. If, as in fig. 21, it be a point of unstable equilibrium, this fact will indicate that the production of the commodity in question on a small scale will not remunerate the producers. So that this production cannot be commenced at all unless some passing necessity has caused temporarily an urgent demand for the commodity of a character similar to that represented by the dotted curve in the figure. But the production, when once fairly started, could be carried on profitably.

§ 7. In discussing the unstable equilibrium which was met with in the theory of foreign trade some remarks were made (Part II. Ch. III. § 7) with regard to the fact that in Economics every event causes permanent alterations in the conditions under which future events can occur. To these the reader is referred. It was argued that in the theory of foreign trade an unstable equilibrium is met with which conforms completely to the conditions which are fulfilled by the unstable equilibrium of mechanics. This case was discussed in connection with curves of Class I., and is illustrated in fig. 4. But it was remarked that these conditions are not completely conformed to by the so-called unstable equilibrium, which depends upon the diminution of the expenses of production that arises from an increase in the amount produced.

It was argued that when any casual disturbance has caused a great increase in the production of any commodity, and thereby has led to the introduction of extensive economies, these economies are not readily lost. Developements of mechanical appliances, of division of labour and of organisation of transport, when they have been once obtained are not readily abandoned. Capital and labour, when they have once been devoted to any particular industry, may indeed become depreciated in value when there is a falling off in the demand for the wares which they produce : but they cannot quickly be converted to other occupations; and their competition will for a time prevent a diminished demand from causing an increased price of the wares. Precisely similar remarks apply to what I have called unstable equilibrium in the present theory: and *mutatis mutandis* they may be reproduced here.

Thus for instance, the shape of the Supply curve in fig. 23 implies that if the ware in question were produced on the scale OV annually, the economies introduced into its production would be so extensive as to enable it to be sold at a price TV. If these economies were once effected the shape of the curve SS' would probably cease to represent accurately the circumstances of supply. The expenses of production, for instance, of an amount OU would no longer be much greater proportionately than those of an amount OV. Thus in order that the curve might again represent the circumstances of Supply it would be necessary to draw it lower down; possibly so much lower as to make it fall into the position of the dotted curve in the figure and make only one intersection with OG. Thus we may lay down a general principle to the effect that if the process by which a ware is manufactured be of such a nature that an increase in the scale of production within certain limits causes great additional increased economies to be introduced into the manufacture, then the Supply curve for the ware between these limits will require some special treatment. For this portion of the curve can only be taken to represent the circumstances of Supply before and up to the occurrence of any event which renders it profitable to produce the commodity on a large scale for a time sufficiently long for the introduction of these economies. After the occurrence of such an event, the curve must be, partially at least, re-drawn. Thus if at a point on OX below this portion of the curve there be drawn in accordance with the rules laid down, an arrow-head pointing to the left; this arrow-head will indicate a resistance that must be overcome before the Amount-index can move to this point. But if by any means the Amount-index is brought to this point, the existence of the arrow-head will not justify us in assuming without investigation that in the corresponding practical problem there will be in operation a force tending to make the Exchange-index move towards the left. Conclusions based upon the assumption of the rigidity of the curves may be applied to practical problems concerning domestic values in so far as the conclusions relate to the resistances which must be overcome before there can be effected an increase in the scale on which cloth or linen is exported: but not in so far as they relate to the forces which may operate to diminish this scale.

Therefore the account of positions of unstable equilibrium which has been deduced from an examination of the curves may not be applied to practical problems generally until a careful enquiry has been instituted in each particular case as to the probability that economies which had once been introduced, would be quickly lost. But though as far as at present appears they cannot be largely used for the immediate deduction of conclusions in matters of practice, there seems to be large scope for the use of them in the suggestion of new practical problems.

§ 8. In applying the curves of Demand and Supply to the solution of any particular problem we must determine definitely what is the length of the period with the average circumstances of which the problem deals. For this purpose much care is required. Even the best writers on Economics have sometimes failed clearly to discriminate the various senses in which they have used the word average in such phrases as "average supply," "average demand," "average value."

Let us consider for instance the case of wheat. The supplies of wheat come almost exclusively from the northern hemisphere, and are therefore harvested at about the same time of year. Consequently if all the facts of the harvest were known, and their bearings properly estimated by all dealers, there need be no important fluctuations in the price of wheat during the year; or at all events none until the prospects of the next harvest had begun to declare themselves. The great fluctuations that do occur even in the winter months, are not to be regarded as the effects of economic causes in the narrower use of the phrase. Their causes are rather to be sought among mental phenomena; in the insufficiency of men's knowledge and the fallibility of men's judgments.

With reference to market prices for markets of long duration some care is required in order to discover the average price or the level about which the market price oscillates. For in comparing prices obtained at two different dates allowance must be made for the interest due on the price obtained at the earlier date. Thus if interest be reckoned at 5 per cent. per annum, the price of 60s. for a quarter of corn sold in January would be on the same level as a price of 61s. 6d. for a quarter sold in the ensuing July.

A list of the monthly prices of wheat since 1793 (Tooke's *History of Prices*, II. p. 390, and *Statistical Abstracts*) exhibits in many cases two oscillations, in some even three, in the course of a single harvest year. Not nearly all these oscillations can be accounted for by variations in the prospects of a good harvest in the coming year. After allowing for these variations and also for the effect of partial and temporary combinations open or tacit among dealers, we find a large margin of irregularities which has to be put to the account of the difficulty of obtaining rapidly the requisite data. This difficulty has been increased by the growing complexity of these data almost as much as it has been diminished by our improved means of transmitting information. It is true that the average price for July for the last 80 years is at least as much in excess as it ought to be—by about 3s. 6d.—of the average price for January. But so tardily are facts ascertained, that when a scanty harvest is followed by an abundant one, not only is the fall in price exhibited in the September column in general comparatively small, but in many cases the progress of the fall is protracted throughout the greater part of the harvest year. For the last 30 years the price has been lower on the average for February than for November; and but little higher for April than for October. The causes that determine the relations of the average price of wheat to the market prices, when the term "average" means average during six winter months, are of an entirely different character from the causes which determine these relations when the period for which the average is taken is long enough to include several harvests.

The periods with which we are concerned in the present discussion are of the latter character. They are sufficiently long to eliminate the casual disturbances which arise from the failure of producers so to adjust the supply to the demand, that the amount supplied may be just sold off at a remunerative price. But they are sufficiently short to exclude fundamental changes in the circumstances of demand and in those of supply. On the side of demand for the ware in question it is requisite that the periods should not include (i) any very great change in the prosperity and purchasing power of the community; (ii) any important changes in the fashions which affect the use of the ware; (iii) the invention or the great cheapening of any other ware which comes to be used largely as a substitute for it; (iv) the deficiency of the supply of any ware for which the ware in question may be used as a substitute, whether this deficiency be occasioned by bad harvests, by war, or by the imposition of customs or excise taxes; (v) a sudden large requirement for the commodity, as e.g. for ropes in the breaking out of a maritime war; (vi) the discovery of new means of utilising the ware, or the opening up of important markets in which it can be sold.

On the side of Supply it is requisite that the periods should not include (i) the opening up or cutting off, as e.g. by a war, or a tax, of any important source of supply of the ware itself or of the material of which it is made; or (ii) the invention of any fundamentally new process or machine for the manufacture of the ware. But the period may include such extended applications of known processes and machinery, and such economies in conveyance and distribution as are direct consequences of an increase in the scale of production.

Thus, to revert to the case of wheat, the supply and demand curves cannot, at all events as applied in the present discussion, be made to exhibit the operation of causes which govern the changes in the value of wheat which have occurred in the course of many generations. Recent controversies render it expedient to examine this point somewhat carefully. British economists have enunciated a Law of Diminishing Return. They assert that a considerable increase in the amount of wheat raised from a given area in a country which is already thickly peopled can be raised only at the cost of an amount of labour increased more than proportionately. American economists assert that in a new country, at all events, and often even in an old country, the growth of population brings with it such improvements in agricultural skill, such new knowledge of processes and implements, such near access to good markets for buying and selling, and such developments of communication by road and railway, that an increased supply of food can be produced at the cost of labour increased less than proportionately. In particular they insist that the amount of labour which has to be expended in order to raise a quarter of wheat under the most unfavourable circumstances in which wheat is grown in England is less than it was many centuries ago. These statements on which British and the American economists severally lay stress are doubtless both true. But they do not traverse one another. The law of diminishing returns may be expressed by a Supply curve for wheat which is throughout inclined positively as in fig. 20. The complementary fact which the special circumstances of America have made prominent may be expressed by a Supply curve for wheat, some portions of which are inclined positively and others negatively, as in fig. 21. It would however be necessary in this case to measure the value of the corn produced in terms of a unit of some particular kind of labour; while in the former case the value may be expressed either in this unit or in terms of a unit of the precious metals. But the two Supply curves thus drawn would correspond to wholly different problems. Each curve would represent changes in the cost, measured in money or labour, of raising corn which would be occasioned by changes in the amount produced. But the former curve would refer to an interval of time so short as to include no fundamental change in the general condition of the country, in the development of the arts of cultivation, of the means of locomotion, and generally of the industries subsidiary to agriculture. Corresponding to this curve there might be drawn a demand curve roughly representing the circumstances of average demand for the wheat during the same period. The position of the point of intersection of the two would then represent approximately the average amount which would be produced and the average price about which the mean price would oscillate. But in the second case

the supply curve would refer to a period so long as to include
fundamental changes in the character of the various industries
of the country. In drawing the curve, allowance would be made
not only for those economies which spring directly from the
increase in the amount produced, but also for those inventions
and other improvements which were caused by the growth of
civilisation that was concurrent with the increase of population.
A supply curve can be thus drawn to express the result of
statistics as to past history or of conjectures as to future history.
But it is obvious that we cannot properly pair this curve off
with a corresponding demand curve, and determine by the
intersection of the two an average value about which the
market value has oscillated.

We might indeed add together the prices of wheat in the
various years, and divide the sum by the number of years, in
order to find an arithmetic mean of the prices. But this mean
would not be rightly called an average result of economic causes.
For such a phrase cannot be strictly interpreted without assuming
some uniformity at least in the general character of the causes
operating. And we could not make any assumption of this kind
which would correspond even approximately to the facts of the
case. Malthus indeed has made[1] some instructive investigations
as to the relations which in the course of English history have
existed between the average price of corn, the average wages of
labor, and the growth of population. It is true that the statistics
at his command were not thoroughly satisfactory, but he made
good use of such as he had; and more recent investigations have
on the whole tended to confirm his conclusions. He concludes,
"that during a course of nearly 500 years the earnings of a
day's labor in this country have probably been more frequently
below than above a peck of wheat; that a peck of wheat may be
considered as something like a middle point, or rather above the
middle point, about which the market wages of labor, varying
according to the demand and supply, have oscillated; and that
the population of a country may increase with some rapidity,
while the wages of labor are even under this point."

But he finds that average corn wages were not far short of
two pecks during the latter part of the fifteenth century, and
that in the seventeenth century they were generally under three
quarters of a peck. "From 1720 to 1750 the price of corn fell
and the wages of labor rose, but still they could command but
little more than the half of what was earned in the fifteenth
century. From this period corn began to rise, and labor not to
rise quite in proportion; but during the forty years from 1770

[1] *Political Economy*, Ch. IV.

to 1810 and 1811, the wages of labor in the command of corn seem to have been nearly stationary."

"It appears then that, making a proper allowance for the varying value of other parts of the wages of labor besides food, the quantity of the customary grain which a laboring family can actually earn, is at once a measure of the encouragement to population and of the condition of the laborer; while the money price of such wages is the best measure of the value of money as far as one commodity can go[1]."

These facts may, perhaps with some little violence to words, be made to represent supply of and demand for employment as determining the average wages of labor. This is how Malthus endeavoured to use them. But they cannot fairly be made to represent the way in which the average price of corn is determined by economic causes.

§ 9. The reader will have no difficulty in drawing for himself diagrams representing the alterations in the curves and in the positions of equilibrium which may arise from any general change in the circumstances either of supply or of demand. The principles on which he will have to proceed are in every respect similar to those on which the investigation of the corresponding problem in the theory of international values has been conducted. We may follow the analogy of the terms used there in describing the alteration of the supply curve which is required when any event causes an increase in the expenses of producing each several amount of the commodity. We may say that such an event, whether it be a tax, or the cutting off of any sources of supply, or any other difficulty, "pushes upwards" the supply curve.

For let P be any point on the curve (fig. 24), so that PM is the price which is necessary to cover the expenses of production of the commodity when the amount OM is produced. Then after the change some larger price pM will be required in order to cover these expenses. Thus as P is made to move along SS', the old supply curve, p will trace out ss', the new supply curve. If the change be the imposition of a tax which bears a fixed ratio to the selling price of the commodity, the ratio of pM to PM will be constant for all positions of P.

Similarly the supply curve may be "pushed downwards" by the remission of a tax or the awarding of a bounty, by the opening up of new sources of supply, or by the invention of an improved method of manufacture. For, as has been said already, any substantially new invention is a change in the circumstances

---

[1] Cairnes, *Leading Principles*, Part I. ch. v. § 3, apparently in ignorance of this investigation and of the conclusive evidence that corn wages have been higher in some centuries than in others, assails the brief reference that Mill has made (*Pol. Econ.* Bk. III. Ch. xv. § 2) to this evidence.

of supply which invalidates the old supply curve. An increase in the scale of production will necessarily lead to increased economies in consequence of the scope which it will offer for the application of already known methods and machinery. In drawing the original supply curve it was assumed that these economies could be predicted; and that allowance could be made for them. But new inventions and other improvements which are not directly caused by an increase in the scale of production are not capable of being predicted; and when they occur they render it necessary to draw a new supply curve from new data.

In the same way the demand curve will be moved upwards by the discovery of any new purpose to which the commodity in question can be applied; and generally by every change that increases the demand for it. A diminution of the demand, arising perhaps from a change in fashion, or from the invention of some substitute for the commodity, will similarly push the demand curve downwards.

It may be noticed that a considerable movement of the supply curve upwards or of the demand curve downwards in fig. 24 will reduce the number of the points of intersection of the curves from three to one; and this one will lie to the left of A. Thus the amount-index may be moved from stable equilibrium at a point vertically below C to a point not very far from O. But it must be remembered that the hypothesis on which this result is obtained does not, generally speaking, correspond to the actual facts of important practical problems. For as has already been argued at length, the indications given by a negatively inclined portion of the supply curve are completely trustworthy only so long as the amount-index is moving under it from left to right; they cease to represent accurately the facts of the corresponding practical problem so soon as this movement has once been made.

CHAPTER II.

§ 1. It has already been insisted that the burden which a tax on a commodity inflicts on the consumers does not consist only of the pecuniary loss which they undergo in paying an increased price for the commodity.

It was argued that the money that they used to expend on the commodity brought in to them a greater satisfaction than they could obtain by expending that money on other things; for if any other mode of expenditure had seemed preferable to them, they would have chosen it. The tax diminishes in two ways the satisfaction which they derive through their facilities for purchasing the commodity. Firstly, in so far as they continue to purchase the commodity, the tax causes them to pay a higher price for it; secondly, the tax deters them from consuming as large an amount of it as before.

In the present chapter a more careful investigation will be given of the amount of this pleasure or satisfaction which a person derives from being able to purchase a particular commodity at a given price; or, in other words, of the amount of the excess or surplus satisfaction which he derives from his purchases of the commodity over the value to him of the money he pays. Now that which a person would be just willing to pay for any satisfaction rather than go without it, is, as will be explained further on, the " economic measure " of the satisfaction to him. The economic measure of that excess or surplus satisfaction into which we are inquiring will be called " Consumers' Rent." Diagrams similar to those of the preceding chapter will be applied in estimating the amount of the total consumers' rent derived by all the several purchasers of the commodity in the market: and in inquiring into the diminution of this consumers' rent which will be caused by a tax on the commodity. It is somewhat difficult to discern clearly the nature of this surplus satisfaction and of its economic measure: but when this difficulty has been overcome, the apparatus of diagrams that is here supplied will be found to be easily handled, and to be capable of achieving important new results.

§ 2.   In order to give definiteness to our notions, let us consider the case of coals purchased for domestic consumption.   Let us assume also for convenience, that it is not practicable to sell less than a ton of coals at a time.   Let us take the case of a man who, if the price of coals were £10 a ton, would just be induced to buy one ton annually; who would just be induced to buy two tons if the price were £7, three tons if the price were £5, four tons if the price were £3, five tons if the price were £2, six tons if the price were £1. 10s., and who, the price being actually £1, does purchase seven tons.   We have to investigate the consumers' rent which he derives from his power of purchasing coal at £1 a ton.

The fact that he would just be induced to purchase one ton if the price were £10, proves that the total enjoyment or satisfaction which he derives from that ton is as great as that which he could obtain by spending £10 on other things.   In other words, the satisfaction derived from, or "the value in use" to him of, a single ton a year, is economically measured by £10. Therefore his power of purchasing one ton of coals for £1 gives him a surplus satisfaction of which the economic measure is £9 in excess of that satisfaction, command over which he gives up by parting with the £1; that is to say, it gives him a consumers' rent of £9.

Again, if the price were £7 a ton, he would just be induced to purchase a second ton; so that the value in use to him of a second ton is measured by £7.   The consumers' rent that he derives from his power of purchasing this ton for £1 is therefore £6 : and so on.   Thus the whole consumers' rent which he derives from the power of purchasing coal at £1 a ton is £9+6+4+2+1+½, i. e. £22½.

We may put the same thing in another way.   The economic measure of the total value in use, or, as Mr Jevons says, of "the total utility of the coal," is the sum of the prices that he would be just willing to give for each successive ton : i. e. £10+7+5+3+2+1½+1, i. e. £29. 10s.   He has to pay for them seven times the value in exchange or market-price of a ton of coal.   This value in exchange is of course equal to the measure of the value in use to him of the last ton of coal which he purchases, or in Mr Jevons' phrase, to the measure of the final utility of a ton of coal to him.   For he will not pay for a thing more than it is worth to him : and if he can get a thing for less than it is worth to him, he will increase his purchases of it.   So that the last ton of coals which he buys, i. e. the ton which he is only just induced to buy, must be worth to him just what he pays for it.

Thus the Consumers' rent measures the surplus or excess of the total value in use to him of the seven tons of coal which he purchases, over the value in use of the commodities which he could have obtained by expending in other ways the £7 which are the value in exchange of those seven tons.

We are as a rule unable to obtain the facts necessary for measuring the value in use of a commodity to any individual who purchases it; for we cannot estimate the quantity which he would purchase at a given price. But, as was argued in the preceding chapter, the statistics of trade will generally enable us to draw the Demand curve of the commodity for the whole market; that is, will enable us to estimate the total amount of the commodity which could be sold at a given price to the whole body of consumers. And by this means we are enabled to find the economic measure of the value in use of the commodity to the several members of the community.

The measure of human satisfaction thus obtained is indeed a rough measure. For in this as in many other portions of economic reasoning it is necessary, as a first approximation, to treat a pleasure that is worth a shilling to one man as equivalent to a pleasure that is worth a shilling to any other man. Assumptions of this nature have indeed to be made in almost every branch of statistical science. For all social and therefore all economic statistics deal with aggregates of human feelings and affections. It is not possible to add together arithmetically any two pleasures without some more or less arbitrary mode of measuring them. Now the economic measure of the satisfaction which a man derives from any source is as has been said the amount of money which he will just give in order to obtain it. The economic measures of various satisfactions can be represented in statistical tables; and these may be used in establishing economic laws[1]. But such laws will contain only a portion of the whole truth of the matter to which they relate. And before deductions from these laws can be used for practical purposes, allowance must be made for the fact that a satisfaction which a rich man values at a shilling is slight in comparison with one for which a poor man will be willing to pay a shilling.

To take an extreme case. Suppose a poor woman who would manage to purchase one pound of tea in a year, even if she had to pay 5s. for it; she will derive vast surplus satisfaction from purchasing several pounds of tea at 2s. a pound.

---

[1] For a more general account of Economic measures the reader is referred to Appendix III.

Then suppose a comparatively rich man who would buy only one bundle of asparagus at the price of 5s. : but who, the price being 2s., purchases several bundles. The surplus satisfaction that the rich man derives from his asparagus at 2s. a bundle is much less than that which the poor woman derives from her power of purchasing tea at 2s. a pound. But the two satisfactions have the same economic measures, in other words the consumers' rents in the two cases are equal. Bearing in mind then that the economic measure of a benefit which the people receive is only a first approximation towards its real importance, we may proceed to estimate the total consumers' rent which is derived from the purchase of a commodity in a market.

The analogy on which the term "consumers' rent" is based is tolerably obvious. The term "rent," or, as we may say, "landlords' rent," is applied to the excess of the value of the total produce of land over the amount which is just required to remunerate the farmer for the outlay involved in raising the produce. So consumers' rent is the excess of the value to a man of the total amount of a commodity which he purchases over the outlay which he has to make in order to obtain it. The farmer endeavours to apply to his land as much capital as can be profitably expended upon it. He expects the last portion of it which he applies, i. e., that portion which he is only just induced to apply, to give a return that at the current price will just remunerate him : he does not expect to obtain from this portion of his outlay any surplus, or rent. So the amount of the outlay made by the purchaser of any commodity is such that the value to him of the last portion of his purchase, i.e. of that portion of the commodity which he is only just induced to buy, is just equal to the value to him of what he pays for it at the current price ; it affords him no surplus or consumers' rent. This analogy will be brought out clearly by a comparison of the diagrams given in this Chapter with those given in the Appendix on rent. But the analogy between the two theories of landlords' rent and of consumers' rent, though close so far as it goes, does not extend far.

§ 3. Let us consider then the demand curve DD' (fig. 25) for a commodity in a given market. Let OH be the amount which is sold there at the price HA annually, a year being taken as the unit of time for the market. Taking any point M in OH let us draw MP vertically upwards to meet the curve in P and cut a horizontal line through A in R. We suppose all the several units of the commodity, say all the tons of coal, to be of like quality ; so that it does not matter which unit is sold to any particular purchaser. It will however be conve-

nient in order to give definiteness to our ideas to suppose the
units numbered in the order of the eagerness of the several
purchasers: the eagerness of the purchaser of any unit being
measured by the price he is just willing to pay for that unit.
The figure informs us that OM units can be sold at the price
PM; but that at any higher price not quite so many units can be
sold.   There must be then some individual who will buy more
at the price PM, than he will at any higher price.   We are
then to regard the OM^{th} unit as sold to this individual.   Suppose for instance that PM represents £2 and that OM represents a million tons.   The purchaser described in the last section was just willing to buy his fifth ton of coal at the price
£2.   The OM^{th} or millionth ton of coal may then be said to be
sold to him.   If AH and therefore RM represent £1, the
consumers' rent derived from the OM^{th} ton is the excess of PM
or £2 which the purchaser of that ton would have been willing
to pay for it over RM the £1 which he actually does pay for it.
Let us suppose that a very thin vertical parallelogram is drawn
of which the height is PM and of which the base is the distance along Ox that measures a single unit or ton of coal.   It
will be convenient henceforward to regard price as measured
not by a mathematical straight line without thickness, as PM;
but by a very thin parallelogram, or as it may be called a thick
straight line, of which the breadth is in every case equal to the
distance along Ox which measures a unit or ton of coal.   Thus
we should say that the total satisfaction derived from the OM^{th}
ton of coal is measured by the thick straight line MP; that
the price paid for this ton is represented by the thick straight
line MR and the consumers' rent derived from this ton by the
thick straight line RP.   Now let us suppose that such thin
parallelograms or thick straight lines are drawn for all positions of M between O and H, one for each ton or unit of coal.
The thick straight lines thus drawn, as MP is, from Ox up to
the demand curve will each measure the total satisfaction
derived from a ton of coal.   The sum of these satisfactions
taken together is the total satisfaction derived from the consumption of coal; and these thick straight lines taken together
occupy and exactly fill up the whole area $DOHA$.   Therefore
we may say that the area $DOHA$ measures the total satisfaction derived from the consumption of coal.   Again each of the
thick straight lines drawn as MR is from Ox upwards as far as
AC represents the price that actually is paid for a ton of coal.
These thick straight lines together make up the area $COHA$:
and therefore this area represents the total price paid for coal.
Finally each of the thick straight lines drawn as RP is from
AC upwards as far as the Demand Curve represents the Con-

sumers' rent derived from the corresponding unit or ton of coal. These thick straight lines together make up the area DCA ; and therefore this area represents the total consumers' rent that is derived from coal when the price is AH.

It has already been remarked that it will seldom be possible to obtain the data necessary for drawing the Demand curve accurately throughout any large portion of its length. If A is the point on the curve corresponding to the amount that is wont to be sold in the market, data may be obtained sufficient for drawing the curve with tolerable correctness for some distance on either side of A; but it will scarcely ever occur that the curve can be drawn with any approach to accuracy right up to D. It happens, however, that the practical applications of this as of other portions of the theory of Domestic values require a knowledge of the shape of the Demand curve only in the neighbourhood of A. At all events in the present discussion we shall not be much concerned to ascertain accurately the total area $DCAD$; it will be sufficient for most of our purposes to know the changes in the magnitude of this area that would be occasioned by moving A through small distances along the curve in either direction. Nevertheless it will be convenient to continue to assume, as in the pure theory we are at liberty to do, that the curve is completely drawn for us[1].

§ 4.　We may proceed to investigate the increase or diminution of Consumers' Rent which will in any particular instance be occasioned by a rise or a fall in the prices at which various amounts of the commodity can severally be produced. According to the phraseology explained at the end of the preceding chapter such a rise or fall will push the supply curve upwards or downwards respectively. An account has already been given of the various causes which may make it necessary to draw a new supply curve. For brevity and for convenience it will be convenient to select from these a tax and a bounty as representing the two classes which may push the supply curve upwards and downwards; and during the present chapter to consider every change in the position of the Supply curve as due either to a tax or to a bounty. The reader will be able at once to make the alterations in the propositions which follow which are necessary in order to adapt them to the case of any other change which may disturb the position of the supply curve.

---

[1] The mathematician will notice that if $y = f(x)$ be the equation to DD' and (a, b) the coordinates of A; the consumers' rent is

$$\int_0^a f(x)\, dx - ab.$$

Let us first consider the effects of the imposition of a tax. Let us commence with the special case in which the expenses of production of the commodity in question are supposed to be independent of the amount produced: or in other words of the special case in which the Supply curve is a horizontal straight line, at all events for some distance on either side of its intersection with the Demand curve. Let then a horizontal straight line CA (figs. 26 and 27) be the supply line before the imposition of the tax. Let the tax be C per unit of the commodity: so that the new supply line is the horizontal straight line ca. Let the Demand curve cut the old and the new Supply lines in A and a respectively, so that A and a are the old and the new positions of equilibrium. Draw AH and ah perpendicular to Ox: let ah cut CA in k. Thus the tax diminishes the Consumers' Rent from the amount DCA to the amount Dca: the loss of the Consumers' Rent is CAa. Also the government collects a tax of Cc on each of Oh, or which is the same thing on each of CK units of the commodity: the total tax which it collects is therefore $cCKa$. The amount which the government receives from the tax is less than the resulting destruction of Consumers' Rent by the amount aKA. In a complete estimate of the total burden which is inflicted on the people by a tax which affords a given revenue to the government, account must be taken of the cost of collection of the tax and of the annoyances and interferences with the freedom of the trade which it occasions. But if these considerations be for the time put aside, we may conclude that the immediate economic effects of the tax will be good or bad according as the loss of Consumers' Rent aKA is, or is not, small as compared with the amount collected $cCKa$. This area aKA may for our present purpose be taken as convertible with the triangle formed by three straight lines joining a, k and A. It is indeed true that if the curve aA be convex towards k the area in question will be less than if aA be concave towards A. But this consideration does not appear to be practically important and it may be hereafter neglected.

We have then to consider the tax to be for our present purposes good or bad according as the triangle aKA is great or small in comparison to the parallelogram $cCKa$; that is according as KA the amount by which the consumption is diminished is small or great in comparison with CK the amount of the remaining consumption. The nature of the demand curve represented in fig. 26 is such that a given rise in price will not induce consumers to curtail their consumption much. The commodity for which this curve is drawn therefore may be a necessary. If not it must be a comfort or a luxury which consumers cannot be easily induced to forego; perhaps because those particular persons who are in the habit of consuming it are wealthy and do not concern themselves about small changes in the expense of their wonted gratifications.   But whatever the commodity be, there is one statement that may be made with certainty with regard to it.   This statement is that there is no available substitute for the commodity which escapes the tax that is imposed on it: or in other words, that the tax in question is not a "discriminating tax."   Thus for example, fig. 26 may perhaps represent the circumstances of the market for butcher's meat in a new country in which an increase in the supply can be obtained without involving an increase in the expenses of production.   Such a tax to whatever other objection it .might be liable would not involve a loss of consumers' rent which would much exceed the receipts of the tax gatherer.   But the effects of a tax levied on mutton and not on beef would be of a wholly different character.   They may be represented by fig. 27, if the Demand curve in that fig. can be taken to represent the various amounts of mutton which it would be possible to dispose of at various prices, the price of beef being assumed to be stationary.   For any considerable increase in the price of mutton under these circumstances would occasion a very great diminution in the consumption of it.   Such a tax therefore would be in effect a discriminating tax.   And it would bring into the state a very small revenue in proportion to the injury that it inflicted on the consumers.

The results thus obtained admit of being explained with sufficient clearness without the aid of diagrams.   But the exact analysis which has just been applied to the simple case in which the Supply curve is a horizontal straight line, was required as an introduction to the more complex cases to which we shall soon proceed.   Before leaving the present simple case, however, it will be well to consider the manner in which the awarding of a bounty on the production of a commodity would affect Consumers' rent.   For this purpose we may use figures 26 and 27, if we take Oc to represent the price at which the commodity would naturally be offered for sale ; and that the awarding of a bounty of cC on the production of each unit of the commodity causes the price to fall to OC.   Let HA and ca be produced to meet in L.   The total bounty which the state will pay, will be Cc on each of OH units of the commodity: it will therefore be represented by the parallelogram $cCAL$. The bounty will have caused Consumers' Rent to increase from the amount Dca to the amount DCA.   So that the increase of Consumers' Rent is measured by the area $cCAa$; and this is less than the total amount of the bounty which the Government pays by the area aLA. Thus if we consider a commodity the expenses of production of which are fixed, that is independent of the amount produced ; we have the following pair of results which are valid independently of all allowances that have to be made on account of the expenses and indirect evils which are involved in collecting a tax or awarding a bounty, viz.:—

A tax on the commodity brings in less to the tax gatherer than it takes from Consumers' Rent; and

A bounty on it takes from the Government more than it adds to Consumers' Rent.

§ 5. We may next examine the change that is made in consumers' rent by a tax on a commodity, the expenses of production of which increase with every increase in the amount produced. This case is represented by pushing the Supply curve in fig. 28 upwards from the position SS' to the position ss'. If the tax be "Specific," i. e., independent of the price of the commodity, the vertical distance between any point on SS' and the corresponding point on ss' will be constant throughout the curves: if the tax be *ad valorem*, this distance will bear a constant ratio to the distance of either point from Ox. But the investigations which follow are independent of any particular assumption as to the principles on which the tax is levied. As before, the position of equilibrium is transferred from A to a; AC and ac are drawn horizontally, $aKEh$ is drawn vertically, cutting AC in k, SS' in E and Ox in h; and EF is drawn perpendicular to Oy. The tax levied on each unit of the commodity is represented by aE; and the total amount of the tax collected is the parallelogram $cFEa$. The loss of consumers' rent is as before $cCAa$. In the preceding case we found that this loss must be greater than the amount collected by the Government. But in the present case the loss of consumers' rent will be less than the total sum which the tax collectors receive if the triangle aKA is less than the parallelogram $CFEK$. As the figure shews, this may easily occur. This result has important practical bearings which will be discussed in a later section.

But bearing in mind that we are here treating of commodities that are produced at home, and not with imported commodities, we must examine the effects which the tax may have upon landlords' rent; that is, upon the rent of the land from which the commodity or the raw material of it is raised. It will be convenient to introduce this examination by first investigating the increase of rent which will follow on an increase in the demand for the commodity, and a consequent rise in its price.

Suppose then that the amount produced is originally Oh

for the production of which Eh is remunerative, and that it
is increased to OH for the production of which AH is required.
Generally speaking, the amount Oh will now be produced with
as little difficulty as before; or even with less if the increase in
the scale of production renders possible improvements in the
methods of production, or in the organization of transport.
The production of the amount hH is a matter indeed of proportionately greater difficulty. But the increase in price is obtained
for the whole amount OH. Whence it follows that this rise in
price must occasion either a higher rate of remuneration to
those who are engaged in the production, or else an increase of
the rent which is obtained by the owners of land or of other natural
agents which may be employed at some stage in the production; or a combination of both these results. No general rule
can be laid down as to the division of the benefits between
these two classes. This division will depend not only upon the
nature of the commodity in question, but also upon the length
of the period for which its average price is estimated. If the
work of production requires specialized skill and habits which
cannot be acquired rapidly, a sudden increase in the amount
produced will necessitate the employment of unhandy workers.
It will be necessary to pay these men well in order to induce
them to enter upon an occupation that is new to them. The
price of the commodity must be sufficient to remunerate the
employers who hire this expensive but unskilled labour. It
must therefore be sufficient to cause a strong competition
among employers, resulting in their offering a very high wage
for skilled labour. This increased wage may itself be regarded
partly as a rent of scarce personal qualities, and partly as exceptionally high profits on the investment of capital in the
technical education of the worker. Similar causes will raise
the "wages of superintendence" of employers and others engaged in the task of management much above their usual level.
Also the profits derived from buildings, machinery, and other
capital specialized to the trade, will be abnormally high. But
the exceptional wages and profits thus obtained by specialized
capital and specialized skill can generally speaking endure only
for a few months or years. So that if we are considering the
causes which determine average prices during long periods of
time, we may suppose that an increase in the demand for the
commodity will occasion sufficient increase in the supplies of
appropriate skill and capital to keep wages and profits down to
their normal level. On this supposition the total expenses
which have to be allowed for on account of the capital and
labour employed in the production of the amount Oh will not
be affected by the fact that an additional amount hH is pro-

duced. The whole of the increase in price from Eh to AH will go as rent to the owner of the land on which the raw material of the commodity is produced.

We may now turn back to the case in which the imposition of a tax causes the amount produced to diminish from OH to Oh; the price which the consumer pays increasing from AH to ah, but the price which the producer receives decreasing from AH to Eh. The skill and capital specialized to the production will be in excess of the requirements of the market and will obtain for a time diminished wages and profits. But gradually the surplus supply of skill and capital will dwindle away, until wages and profits rise to their normal level. So that if the periods of time for which we are making our calculations are long we may say that the total expenses which have to be allowed for on account of the capital and labour employed in the production of the amount Oh will not be affected by the fact that the amount hH is no longer produced. The whole of the diminution in the price which the producer receives from AH to Eh will fall upon the owner of the land on which the raw material of the commodity is produced.

In fact there is a certain class of problems referring to agricultural produce in which the total landlords' rent will be measured before the imposition of the tax by CSA, and afterwards by FSE.

For let us make the supposition that the expenses which have to be allowed for capital and labour on account of the production of any given unit of the commodity, as, e.g., the Oh^{th}, are not affected by the fact that additional units are produced. That is to say the expenses of production exclusive of rent of the Oh^{th} unit will be a fixed amount hE. Therefore, when the price HA, that is hK, is obtained for this unit, the landlord will be able to claim as his share that portion EK of the vertical line hK which is intercepted between the Supply curve and the price line CA. Applying to this case the same method of reasoning that has been applied above to the case of consumers' rent we find that the total landlords' rent is measured by the sum of those vertical thick lines corresponding to successive units of the commodity up to the OH^{th}, which are intercepted between the Supply curve and the price line CA. And the sum of these thick lines exactly makes up the area CSA.

On this supposition the tax diminishes landlords' rent by the amount $FEAC$. This together with $cCAa$, the loss of consumers' rent, makes up the whole area $cFEAa$, which exceeds the total receipts of the tax gatherer by the amount EAa.

This method of measuring landlords' rent illustrates the analogy which exists between it and consumers' rent. It is possible to erect by this method an apparatus of curves which shall contain a complete exposition of the pure theory of the rent of land. But another apparatus of curves which is practically more convenient for this purpose is supplied in an Appendix to the present volume.

As in the previous case we may represent the results of awarding a bounty to the production by supposing that SS' is the original position of the Supply curve and that in consequence of the bounty it is pushed downwards into the position ss' (see fig. 29). Let ha be produced to meet SS' in L and let LG be drawn perpendicular to Oy. The bounty will have caused the amount produced to increase from OH to Oh, the price to the consumer to decrease from HA to ha, and the expenses of production to increase from HA to hL. The total bounty paid by Government will be cG on each of OH units of the commodity: and will be represented by the area $GcaL$. It will thus be necessarily much larger than the increase of consumers' rent, which will be only $CcaA$.

But here again allowance must be made for the increase that the bounty would occasion in landlords' rent. We have just seen that in the case of agricultural produce we may suppose the Supply curve SS' to be so drawn that when the price is HA the total landlords' rent is represented by the area CSA. On this supposition the total landlords' rent after the awarding of the bounty will be represented by the area GSL; that is, it will be increased by the area $GCAL$. Thus the increase of consumers' rent together with the increase of landlords' rent will be less than the total bounty which Government pays by the area LAa. If the commodity in question had been an imported commodity the increased price which was required to obtain an increased supply would in general have been a benefit to the foreign producer at the expense of the consumer at home. The Government by levying a tax would intercept some of this benefit, but as has been already indicated it could not in general intercept much of it. A more full examination of this matter is given elsewhere.

§ 6. We have lastly to consider the case in which the Supply curve is inclined negatively in the neighbourhood of A, its points of intersection with the Demand curve. That is to say, we have to suppose that the greater be the amount produced, the less will be the expenses of production; provided this amount be neither much greater nor much less than that amount OH which actually is produced when the trade is undisturbed. The figure (fig. 30) may be constructed as before. The Supply curve is pushed upward by the tax to the position ss', and cuts DD' in a: ah drawn vertically cuts SS' in E. The total

receipts of the tax gatherer are represented as before by the area
$cFEa$: and the loss of Consumers' Rent is represented by the
much larger area $cCAa$. The diminution of the demand for
the raw material of the manufacture will probably cause some
diminution of landlords' rent. We must remember the indications given by such portions of the Supply curve as are inclined
negatively are not completely trustworthy when they relate to
movements of the amount-index towards the left, as in the present case. We must remember that the tax may act tardily
in crushing out such economies as have already been introduced
into the manufacture. But when every due allowance has been
made, it will remain true that a tax imposed on a commodity
for which the Supply curve is inclined negatively, involves a
wasteful destruction of Consumers' Rent.

We may as before represent the results of awarding a
bounty to the production by supposing that ss' is the original
position of the Supply curve ; and that in consequence of the
bounty it is pushed down into the position SS'. Thus the
amount-index will move to the right from h to H ; and the
indications given by the curve may be trusted. Let HA be
produced as before to meet SS' in L, then the total bounty
paid by the Government is represented by the area $GCAL$; and
the gain of Consumers' Rent by the area $cCAa$; the latter area
will often be, as it is in the figure before us, much larger than
the former area. Moreover, allowance must be made for an
increase of landlords' rent which may have accrued from ac
increased demand for the raw material of the manufacture. For
the increased demand for the raw material will probably have
caused its price to rise ; at the same time that, in consequence
of the economies introduced into the manufacture, it causes the
price of the finished product to fall.

Fig. 31 represents a remarkable, though of course also an
exceptional, instance of the case, a less striking instance of
which is represented in fig. 30. If the awarding of a bounty
push downward the Supply curve from the position SS' into the
position S_1S_1', equilibrium would pass from A to A_1; and from
A_1 it might probably pass to C_1, on the occasion of some temporary increase in demand. If the Supply curve be pushed
downward into the position S_2S_2', equilibrium will necessarily
pass to C_2, and thus an enormous increase of Consumers' Rent
will be effected by a bounty, the total cost of which to Government will not be very great.

§ 7. If we compare the results of the last three sections, we
shall obtain a conclusion of great importance. Let us suppose
then that figs. 28 and 30 are drawn to the same scale. That is,
let the distances along Ox_1 which represent units of the com-

modity, be equal in the two figures; and let the distances along Oy, which represent any given price, be equal in the two figures : so that equal areas represent equal sums of money in the two figures. Let us suppose also that the area $cFEa$ in fig. 28 is just equal to the area $GCAL$ in fig. 30; so that Government by levying a tax of cF in fig. 28 on each unit of the commodity represented there would obtain the means of awarding the bounty of CG in fig. 30 on each unit of the commodity represented in that figure. It would thus diminish Consumers' Rent by $cCAa$ in fig. 28, and would increase it by the much larger area $cCAa$ in fig. 30. It is true that the tax in fig. 28 will have caused a diminution of land-lords' rent; but this will not necessarily be much greater than that increase of landlords' rent which will arise from the in-creased demand for the raw material of the manufacture in fig. 30. It is, however, possible to suppose that the loss of landlords' rent in the one case is considerably greater than the gain in the second; it is possible also to make liberal allowance for the cost of working of the Government departments that manage the collection of the tax and the awarding of the bounty; and yet to conclude that by the scheme in question Government may have conferred a great economic benefit on the nation as a whole.

But before a practical rule be based upon this result of the pure theory, it is necessary to take account of other classes of considerations. For the purposes of pure theory we have been at liberty to argue as though the knowledge and the probity of Government were unlimited. We have assumed that Go-vernment knowledge is sufficient to enable it to draw the Sup-ply and Demand curves for the commodities in question; or at least such portions of the curves as lie in either figure between ah and AH. Thus we have assumed Government not only to know the present circumstances of the markets for various com-modities, but also to forecast changes in the expenses of produc-tion which would result from changes in the amount produced. We have also assumed that Government officials will not be in any manner imposed upon or corrupted by those who desire to avoid the payment of the tax, or to obtain the bounty. The practical statesman, before venturing on such a scheme as that here suggested, will have to take account not only of the mis-haps that may arise from errors in his calculations, but also of the deterioration of public morals which is likely to ensue when it is to the interest of wealthy classes of producers to bribe legislators or public officers. He will also have to take account of the injustice which may be involved in taxing one set of con-sumers in order to give a bounty to another. But it should

always be observed that a single tax cannot rightly be con-
demned as unjust; such a condemnation can attach only to
a system of taxation taken as a whole.

§ 8. It has just been argued that Consumers' Rent may
possibly be increased by the plan of bringing a tax on some
commodities in order to provide the means of awarding a
bounty on others; but that such a scheme would be likely to
work mischief indirectly. The analysis of the present chapter
leads us, however, to a practical result of great importance: for
we have seen that a much larger destruction of Consumers'
Rent will be involved in levying a given amount of revenue by
taxes on commodities of which the expenses of production
diminish as the amount produced increases, as in fig. 30, than
by taxes on those for which the opposite rule holds, as in
fig. 28. It is true that the destruction of landlords' rent is
likely to be somewhat greater in the latter case than in the
former; but it will not in general be much greater. Consequently it appears that account being taken of the interests
of consumers and landlords together, it is not expedient that
the revenue should be derived from taxes levied equally on all
commodities; but that such revenue as is derived from taxes on
commodities should be obtained almost exclusively from commodities the expenses of production of which increase, or at
least do not diminish, as the amount produced increases.

The whole of a man's income is expended in the purchase of
services and of commodities. It is indeed commonly said that
a man spends some portion of his income and saves another.
But it is a familiar economic axiom that a man purchases
labour and commodities with that portion of his income which
he saves just as much as he does with that which he is said to
spend. He is said to spend when he seeks to obtain present
enjoyment from the services and the commodities which he
purchases. He is said to save when he causes the labour and
the commodities which he purchases to be devoted to the production of wealth from which he expects to derive the means of
enjoyment in the future. It is possible to devise a plan by
which taxes on raw materials and implements and on finished
commodities and personal services should be so adjusted as
to take from each man the same percentage of his total income.
But such a plan will be complex, and it would involve too long
a digression to investigate it here. Moreover, all economists
are agreed that it would be expedient, if it could practically
be done, to exempt from taxation that portion of a man's income
which he saves. They would prefer to levy taxes only on the
remainder of his income; or, as we may hereafter say, in conformity to popular usage, only "on his expenditure." And it is

obvious that such a tax would be convertible with a tax levied equally on every percentage taken by taxation from every sum which he expends on the purchase of labour or commodities for his own immediate consumption and not for the purposes of trade. Next it is obvious that the analysis of the Consumers' Rent which has been applied to the demand for and supply of commodities of any kind may be applied with only verbal alterations to the demand for and the supply of services of any kind. A Demand curve for any class of services may be drawn on just the same principles as Demand curves for any commodity. And when the market-price of such services is known, the Consumers' Rent which accrues to the purchasers of them is determined in just the same manner as before. We arrived recently at the conclusion that it is not expedient that the revenue should be derived from taxes levied equally on all commodities. We now see that this principle may be extended: but the enunciation of it in its extended form is a matter of some difficulty. We must in this case also commence by putting aside for the present all considerations relating to the expenses and other difficulties involved in collecting. We have then to compare the advantages of two systems of taxation in each of which taxes are levied on all purchases, commodities and services which are designed to afford gratification directly, and are not made in the course of trade or intended to be used as capital. According to the first system, a certain amount of revenue is supposed to be collected exclusively from commodities the expenses of production of which increase as the amount produced increases. According to the second, the same revenue is collected by taxes on all purchases of commodities and services for the purposes of direct gratification. We find that the first system is more advantageous than the second: that the second is convertible with what we have called a tax upon expenditure : and since this tax has unquestionably superior advantages to those possessed by an income-tax, we obtain the important result that the expenses and other difficulties of collection being neglected, the first system of taxation is more advantageous than an income-tax.

This principle does not prove that on the whole an income-tax is inexpedient. For in levying other taxes customs and excise officers are compelled, as has been already observed, to worry and hamper by their inspection the trader and the producer. Moreover, they levy the tax in the first instance from capital that is being productively employed, and the consumer is compelled ultimately to pay not only the amount of the tax, but also a high rate of interest, or traders' profits upon it. The income-tax evades these evils ; and though the income-tax assessments cannot in the present state of public morality be made with tolerable accuracy, there is no reason why public opinion should not be gradually so acted upon as to enable the tax to be levied equitably. The general tenor of the arguments of the present treatise points to the conclusion that every effort should be made thus to act upon public opinion with the purpose of ultimately raising nearly the whole of the revenue by direct taxation.

But the principle that has just been laid down is subversive of one particular that has not been unfrequently urged in favour of the substitution of an income-tax for taxes on particular commodities.

This argument is, that if each man's contribution is taken from him directly in the form of an income-tax, the Government leaves it entirely to his own discretion to decide what commodities or other sources of satisfaction to himself he can most conveniently give up in order to obtain the means of paying the tax. But that Government wantonly infringes individual liberty if it levies taxes on particular commodities, with the effect of inducing the individual to curtail his consumption of them rather than of others. It is urged that in so doing Government claims for itself the power of judging better than the individual can, what is the relative value to him of the various gratifications which he purchases.

This argument is fallacious because it takes no account of the fact that every individual, and therefore the whole state, has a direct interest in the character of each man's expenditure. For brevity let us suppose A to be a commodity the expenses of production of which continually increase as the amount produced increases: and B to be a commodity for which the opposite law holds. Then if a person increases his purchases of B, he helps to increase the scale on which it is produced, and thus to lower its price; so that he confers a benefit on all others who may wish to consume B. But if he increases his purchases of A, his action tends to raise the price of A, he injures those who desire to purchase A. By purchasing A rather than B, he will probably add more to landlords' rent in one direction than he takes from it in another, but not in general much more. Therefore it would be to the interests of the state that each man should be directed to devote less of his income to the purchase of A and more to the purchase of B than he would if he took no account of the interest of any person except himself in the matter.

We are not at present concerned to estimate the probability that any Government will possess sufficient knowledge, judgment and power to enable it to perform such a task with any

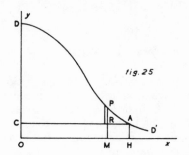

fig. 25

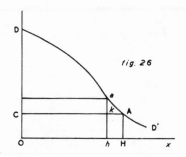

fig. 26

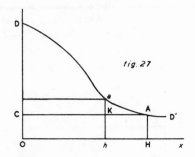

fig. 27

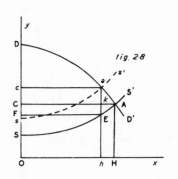

fig. 28

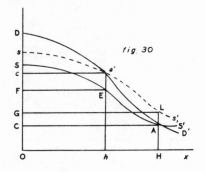

fig. 30

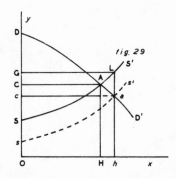

fig. 29

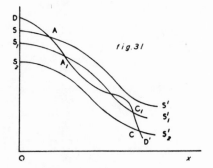

fig. 31

tolerable success. It is sufficient to establish here that a Government which should levy its revenues by a tax on income or expenditure would cut itself off from the attempt to use a power which it theoretically has of promoting the common weal. Theoretically it has the power of so adjusting taxation as to cause each individual on the one hand to contract his consumption of those commodities, a diminution of the demand for which will benefit those who continue to purchase them; and on the other hand, somewhat to augment his consumption of those commodities, an increase in the total demand for which will lower the price at which they can be produced.

COMMENTARY

Pure Theory of Foreign Trade

Page 2. The footnote reference to Appendix I probably refers to part of the original document not printed by Sidgwick (see Editorial Note). In all probability, the material contained in this Appendix had already been published in Marshall's essay "On Mr. Mill's Theory of Value".[1] (Reprinted in *Memorials of Alfred Marshall*, p. 119.) This conjecture is reinforced by the reference to an Appendix on Mill's Theory of Value contained in *Pure Theory of Domestic Values*, p. 7.

Page 11, line 32. "Prop. IV" should read "Prop. VI".

Page 20, lines 8 and 12. No indication has been found of the positions of P′, P″, or P‴ on Fig. 7.

Fig. 13. This figure is not referred to in the text but it has been reproduced in Appendix I of *Money Credit and Commerce* (p. 356). This indicates that the missing portions of the work on international trade (Props. XIV–XVI, see p. 24 of this essay and p. 4 of *The Pure Theory of Domestic Values*) probably covered the theory of import taxes and other influences changing the shape of the curves contained in sections 5–7 of that Appendix. However, it must be remembered that the concept of elasticity was first adopted by Marshall in "The Graphic Method of Statistics" read to the International Statistical Conference in 1885 (reprinted in *Memorials*, p. 175).

Pure Theory of (Domestic) Values
It is interesting to note that, in one copy at least, Marshall substituted in the title the word "Inland" for "Domestic".

Page 5, line 26. "either . . . or" should read "neither . . . nor".

Page 10, footnote "§ 9" should be "§ 5".

Page 11, line 20. "equilibrium" should be inserted after "unstable".

Page 11, line 25. "Prop. XIV" should be "Prop. XIX".

Page 12, line 18. "Part II, Ch. III, § 7" obviously refers to Ch. II, § 7 of *Pure Theory of International Trade*.

Page 13, line 12. "OG" should be "DD′ ".

Page 22, footnote. The material contained in this Appendix was probably reproduced in Notes VI, VII, VIII and (perhaps) IX of the mathematical Appendix to *Principles of Economics*. It should be noted that this Appendix is numbered "III" and the only other Appendix number referred to is "I". (See *Pure Theory of Foreign Trade*, p. 2.) This would indicate that an Appendix originally intended for publication is missing, although it may be the Appendix on Rent referred to first on p. 23.

---

(1) *Fortnightly Review*, Vol. XIX, C.XII, Apr. 1876, pp. 591-602.

Page 23, line 35. No clear indication of the contents of this Appendix can be gathered from the text. (See also p. 31, line 3.)

The references to rectangular hyperbolæ (in the complete footnote to the Preface of the first edition of *Principles of Economics*, referred to in the Editorial Note to this edition) and the "apparatus of curves" (see p. 31) might indicate that Marshall used equal outlay curves in this Appendix. This view is strengthened by his use of these curves in his outline of the theory of consumers' surplus in *Principles* (Figs. 36 and 37, pp. 488 and 490).

Page 26, line 9. "C" should be "Cc".

Page 26, line 16. "CAa" should be "CAac".

Page 27, line 40. This construction was not contained in the diagrams included in the original edition of these papers. However, the required additions are quite clear from the text.

G. S. DORRANCE